Liven Up
Your
Library

*Design Engaging and
Inclusive Programs
for Tweens and Teens*

Valerie Tagoe and Julia E. Torres

International Society for Technology in Education
PORTLAND, OREGON • ARLINGTON, VIRGINIA

Liven Up Your Library
Designing Engaging and Inclusive Programs for Tweens and Teens
Valerie Tagoe and Julia E. Torres

Acquisitions Editor: *Valerie Witte*
Editor: *Emily Reed*
Copy Editor: *Angela Wade*
Proofreader: *Laura Gibson*
Indexer: *Angela B. Wade*
Book Design and Production: *Kim McGovern*
Cover Design: *Beth DeWilde*

Library of Congress Cataloging-in-Publication Data
Names: Tagoe, Valerie, author. | Torres, Julia E., author.
Title: Liven up your library : design engaging and inclusive programs for tweens and teens / Valerie Tagoe and Julia E. Torres.
Description: Portland, Oregon : International Society for Technology in Education, [2022] | Includes bibliographical references and index.
Identifiers: LCCN 2022008670 | ISBN 9781564849090 (paperback) | ISBN 9781564849069 (epub) | ISBN 9781564849083 (pdf)
Subjects: LCSH: Libraries and students--United States. | Libraries and teenagers--United States. | Libraries and schools—United States. | Libraries and community—United States. | School libraries—Activity programs. | Young adults' libraries—Activity programs. | School libraries—Services to minorities. | School librarian participation in curriculum planning.
Classification: LCC Z718.7 T34 2022 | DDC 027.62/6--dc23/ eng/20220412
LC record available at https://lccn.loc.gov/2022008670

First Edition
ISBN: 978-1-56484-909-0
Ebook version available

Printed in the United States of America

ISTE® is a registered trademark of the International Society for Technology in Education.

About ISTE

The International Society for Technology in Education (ISTE) is home to a passionate community of global educators who believe in the power of technology to transform teaching and learning, accelerate innovation and solve tough problems in education.

ISTE inspires the creation of solutions and connections that improve opportunities for all learners by delivering: practical guidance, evidence-based professional learning, virtual networks, thought-provoking events and the ISTE Standards. ISTE is also the leading publisher of books focused on technology in education. For more information or to become an ISTE member, visit iste.org. Subscribe to ISTE's YouTube channel and connect with ISTE on Twitter, Facebook and LinkedIn.

Digital Age Librarians Series

This series written for librarians by librarians features books focused on topics important to media specialists/teacher librarians.

Explore Other Books in the Series

Reimagining Library Spaces: Transform Your Space on Any Budget (2017) by Diana Rendina
> This practical guide shares tips for affordably transforming library spaces, how-tos for hosting makerspaces and learning labs, and suggestions for supporting BYOD.

Connected Librarians: Tap Social Media to Enhance Professional Development and Student Learning (2017) by Nikki D Robertson
This engaging book provides the professional development librarians need to understand how to use social media effectively to improve student learning.

Inspiring Curiosity: The Librarian's Guide to Inquiry-Based Learning (2018) by Colette Cassinelli
This practical guide for secondary school librarians details how to collaborate with teachers and students to develop inquiry-based research projects.

Leading from the Library: Help Your School Community Thrive in the Digital Age (2019) by William Bass and Shannon McClintock Miller
Written by a seasoned librarian and an education leader, this book guides librarians in becoming leaders in their school communities, with strategies on developing partnerships, empowering students, and more.

For a curated collection of ISTE resources for librarians, visit iste.org/Librarians.

About the Authors

Valerie Tagoe (@bookmarksllc) is a high school librarian in Texas. She's a winner of the S. Janice Kee Award from Texas Woman's University and a past president of the Dallas Association of School Librarians. Currently, she's a member of the Young Adult Library Services Association (YALSA) board of directors. In addition to serving on the board, Tagoe is also active in the Texas Library Association (TLA). She holds a bachelor's in French, with a minor in History, from the University of Oklahoma; a master's of bilingual education from Southern Methodist University; and an MLS from Texas Woman's University.

Julia E. Torres (@juliaerin80) is a language arts teacher and librarian in Denver, Colorado. An advocate for all students and public education, Torres is a frequent conference and event speaker, and facilitates workshops and professional conversations about equity, anti-bias/anti-racist education, culturally sustaining pedagogies, and literacy in the digital age. She is a current member of the Amelia Elizabeth Walden Award Committee, a 2020 Library Journal Mover and Shaker, and a past president of the Colorado Language Arts Society (a regional affiliate of the National Council of Teachers of English). She holds a master's of education in secondary education curriculum and instruction from University of Phoenix, a master's in creative writing from Regis University, and a master's in library and information science from the University of Denver.

Acknowledgments

I would like to thank Dr. Cynthia Charles, LaMoya N. Burks, kYmberly Keeton, and Kiera O'Shea Vargas J.D. for sharing their insights on librarianship. I would also like to thank the librarians who shared their experiences with programming.

This book is dedicated to my parents, Seth and Mabel, and to the Tagoe, Mills, and Dodoo families for the love, encouragement to achieve, and support you have given me, and for showing me how to welcome and help others. I would also like to dedicate this book to the excellent teachers, librarians, and school administrators—like Ms. Clark-McCoy, Ms. Nancy Toney, Ms. Olivia Henderson, and Mr. Marcus Johnson—who have been an example and an inspiration to me as an educator. I would also like to dedicate this book to the students of Woodrow Wilson High School in Dallas, TX. Your ideas and creativity helped to inspire me as a librarian to create innovative programs and opened my eyes to the unique potential and impact that librarians have on instruction, learning, and student achievement.

—Valerie

I would like to thank my mother Deborah, the first librarian in my life and the most knowledgeable book recommender I've ever known. Thanks to Dr. Jung Kim, Dr. Sarah Park Dahlen, Edith Campbell, Julie Stivers, Jillian Heise, Angie Manfredi, Mary Thomas, and Ashleigh Rose for always being open to collaboration and for being some of the first to welcome me into the brilliant and beautiful world of librarianship. I would also like to thank my Educolor familia for being just that—through it all.

For my children, Trenton and Josie, who have shared their mother with the world, continuously cheered me on, brought me snacks, and caused a continual ruckus behind the laptop screen. I love you; you are my sun, moon, and stars. To HJA, MAF, and DMH for believing in me and this project from the beginning and for being my guides on the other side. I would also like to dedicate this book to Gladys and Will, who foresaw the potential for this project years before I ever even had the idea I would be writing a book. Last, but certainly not least, I'd like to dedicate this book to my "Soul Family" from the Montbello Campus: Zach, Arnetta, Duval, Juanita, Sara, Eno, and Obi, and from Denver Public Schools Ed Tech & Library Services, Janet Damon and Caroline Hughes, without whom none of my work would have begun in the first place.

—Julia

Contents

Foreword... xi

Introduction... 1

The Need for Inclusive Library Programming................................1
Our Stories..2
What You'll Find in This Book 3

CHAPTER 1
Programming as Praxis.. 5

Effective Library Programming for Tweens and Teens 5
Start with the Why..7
Standards and Library Programming 9
Who Has the Time?... 14
Reimagining Library Legacies... 16
Be Flexible.. 22
Key Points... 23
Reflection... 24

CHAPTER 2
Everyone Is Welcome 25

A Philosophy for Creating a Welcoming Environment......................... 26
Culturally Relevant Librarianship... 29
Library Skills for a Lifetime 36
Be Flexible.. 41
How to Create a Culturally Responsive Library Space 44
Perspectives from College Librarians 51
Key Points... 57
Reflection... 58

CHAPTER 3
Making It Work 59

Standards or No Standards: That Is the Question 60
Show Me the Money 61

Contents

STEAM and Makerspaces 66

Marketing and Library Program Advocacy 68

Get Creative 76

Sustaining a Library Program for Everyone 80

Key Points 80

Reflection 82

CHAPTER 4

The Program Is Done ... Now What? 83

Advocacy 86

Program Evaluation and Assessment 88

Creating Assessments for Programming 94

Bringing It All Together 96

Mentorship 97

Key Points 102

Reflection 103

CHAPTER 5

Programming Ideas & Curriculum Connections 105

Practical Programming Template 106

Considerations for Certified Teacher Librarians 108

Considerations for School Library Staff 109

Media Literacy for a New Era 112

Teen Advisory Councils 116

Book Clubs 121

Book Reviews and Expanding Your Circle of Community 124

Literacy Instruction 126

Advocacy Matters 127

Conclusion 129

Key Points 130

Reflection 131

References 132

Index 135

Foreword

Dr. Desiree Alexander

Libraries have undergone a revolution! Gone are the days when the library was only a place where quiet contemplation happened and the only reason to open its doors was to check out a book. Even though contemplation and checking out books are still good reasons to visit, libraries are now the epicenter of where fun, engaging learning and collaboration happens. These spaces have become the thriving, beating hearts of school campuses and communities as they have transformed into learning spaces where everyone is welcome to come explore who they are and who they want to be. Patrons can take adventures through books, build STEAM projects, construct in makerspaces, and learn about the world around them.

Another way libraries have been revolutionized is through programming. Some of my favorite memories of being a school librarian are creating programs for my students, teachers, parents, and community members. I learned so much about the thoughts, hearts, and culture of those I served and how to create programs that were fun, inclusive, engaging, and educational specifically for them. Programming helped me see my patrons and community in a different light and helped them to see our library as a place created for them.

What I love about this book is that it is for every librarian, whether you are just getting started with programming or are a seasoned pro. Throughout the book, the reader learns why programming is critically important while also gaining practical, credible ideas to plan those programs. In each chapter, the reader gets key points and reflections on how these programs will positively affect their library and surrounding community. The chapters are relevant, current, and give plenty of resources that will help librarians implement their own programming ideas successfully!

Valerie Tagoe and Julia Torres truly understand the struggles of the library science field and realize the need for programming to fit into the various roles librarians are asked to fill. They not only give examples of programs you can do tomorrow but personalize their advice for various types of librarians and their duties. One example of this is making sure each librarian starts with his/her/their why. Understanding why you want to program and how it benefits your population is the start of setting up your library programming for success. They go on to explain how librarian standards (AASL, ISTE, and Future Ready) are celebrated through programming and how even your noncurricular programs still fit into your standards. The reader learns directly from other current librarians through interviews and dissects how to make their library (and library programming) culturally relevant by getting students and other patrons involved in the programming itself.

This book is the omnibus on library programming I wish I'd had when I was in the library. It is your one-stop guide to answer the questions of what programming is, who should program, when to program, how to program, and the ever-important why program. This is the call to action you need to motivate you to either start programming today or continue with your programs by making them more engaging and more inclusive. Having standards, resources, examples, and practical advice all in one place creates the guidebook every librarian will want and need to have on hand and in their library collection!

Take the first step toward creating engaging, relevant, and inclusive programs by diving into this book. Then share your journey, and your successful programs with other librarians to further the impact. Remember, together we can, and together we will!

— Dr. Desiree Alexander is founder and CEO of Educator Alexander Consulting and deputy director of the Associated Professional Educators of Louisiana.

Introduction

The Need for Inclusive Library Programming

Librarians and libraries of all types (school, public, college, and university) are in the perfect position to advance learning through programming due to flexible spaces, knowledge and backgrounds of staff, collections, and community connections. The communities we serve and the needs of those we serve are always changing. Tween and teen populations are becoming more diverse; therefore the programs we provide and how we craft them must also change.

Recently, and particularly since spring 2020, we have seen protests against injustice; a racial reckoning in America; and the COVID-19 pandemic and its economic, health, social, and political effects. With all that is happening in the world, librarians see firsthand that our programs and services are sorely needed and are vital to help bridge the digital divide and close the achievement gaps that exist for students so they may have a bright future.

Libraries are places where individuals can and do come together to have collective experiences around making things, hearing and sharing beloved stories, and building communities. When we are intentional about using library spaces to fuel the pursuit of justice, rather than using them merely as places to house and organize information, we claim our space in the long line of those who continuously strive for a better, freer, more humanitarian society.

School and public libraries can serve as true tools for the development of liberatory consciousness in a society that has become increasingly more interconnected. Our liberation is inextricably linked, and we know that, as many have said before, "Nobody is free until we are all free."

Our Stories

Valerie has experience working in both school and public libraries that serve diverse teen populations. She finds that programming allows librarians to advance learning in creative and innovative ways. It is imperative that librarians develop relationships with and gain input from *all* teens in their communities, keep pace with changes in technology, and are knowledgeable about culture, curricular needs, and information needs of the communities they serve in order to create innovative programming. It may take a small start: piloting some program ideas with a small group, then bringing those ideas to scale. She encourages librarians not to be apprehensive about doing things a different way or taking an unconventional approach.

Julia has experience in secondary education settings. She has served as a language arts educator for almost twenty years, and though she is new to librarianship, her praxis has always prioritized reading as a fundamental part of cultivating environments where young people can thrive. Julia's library was one where young people learned about empowerment, social justice, and intersectional identities, and trusted that adults in the community valued and prioritized their stories, as well as those of times past.

One of the most important lessons of librarianship learned during the experience of writing this book has been that we cannot claim to serve young people while excluding them from conversations and decision-making about resources and materials that are primarily for their use. We must always prioritize and protect student empowerment as a key right and responsibility when working with young people.

What You'll Find in This Book

Chapter 1: Programming as Praxis examines why library programming is done and how to align standards and manage program planning.

Chapter 2: Everyone Is Welcome describes the importance of not only welcoming teens to the library but activating teen engagement and student agency, as well as insights into culturally relevant librarianship.

Chapter 3: Make It Work shares practical advice on how programs can be made manifest by securing funding, along with steps for marketing programs to teens.

Chapter 4: The Program Is Done ... Now What takes a look at program evaluation and assessment, and presenting the evaluation and assessment data to stakeholders and grant-makers, as well as using data as a means for library advocacy.

Chapter 5: Practical Programming Ideas explores some program ideas that librarians can adapt and put into practice now, as well as tips and resources to help get the job done.

Features throughout the book include:

- Interviews and input solicited from practicing librarians as it pertains to various elements of each chapter.
- "We Do This in Community" examples that detail ways to expand library programming beyond a physical space and by including key stakeholders.

- QR codes and links to online resources that transform thinking, as well as practical materials for use that support the concepts in each chapter.

- Reflection questions for consideration as individuals or as part of a system-wide book study.

This book also ties in the importance of connecting or aligning library programming to ISTE and AASL standards, as well as state standards, particularly when it comes to selling or promoting programs to stakeholders, such as school principals and other stakeholders who review student performance data and approve funding for libraries. Principals and other stakeholders are always looking for ways to continuously improve student achievement and make recommendations with that goal in mind.

CHAPTER 1

Programming as Praxis

Library programming at its core is a series of specialized events or learning experiences. Ideally, programming is culturally relevant and tailored to the needs and interests of the patrons, whether they are first-year college students, young adults, or adolescents just starting their journey into secondary school.

Effective Library Programming for Tweens and Teens

Programming for teens and young adults is a catalyst for learning and exploration. It is also where we see practice and pedagogy come together—a term education practitioners refer to as "praxis." Library programming activities and learning experiences should pique students' interests, capture their imaginations, and advance and deepen their learning.

Piquing Interests of Students

Programming should appeal to tweens and teens and their interests. For example, if your teen student population is already part of the workforce, working part-time in a myriad of sectors, a program on creating a winning resume for the workforce and college or a Get Interview Ready program may pique their interests. The librarian can not only instruct them on how to craft a winning resume but also show them technology tools they can use to build a resume, guide them to advice on how to prepare for an interview, and suggest resources that will assist them further. After you complete the programming reflection piece at the beginning of this chapter, you may have ideas of what will pique the interests of students and patrons at your library.

Capturing the Imagination

Library programming should capture students' imaginations and generate new ideas or new questions of inquiry. Aspire to create programming in which tweens and teens will walk away inspired to imagine, think of possibilities, and ask new questions. As a librarian, you can guide students in the right direction to further explore the subjects and topics that have captured their imaginations. Capturing the imagination can lead to new discovery and new learning.

Inquiry is a major part of instruction, particularly in Advanced Placement and International Baccalaureate courses, as inquiry is taught from elementary with the primary and middle year programs and then continued through high school when students take on writing the extended essay. Students often select topics that have captured their imagination and that they wish to research further, which leads to the next component of effective programming: advancing and deepening learning.

Advancing and Deepening Learning

All libraries can serve as the place where teens can advance and deepen their learning through programming. According to its mission statement, the Zula B. Wylie Public Library in Cedar

Hill, Texas, seeks to "be the community place that acts as the Door to Discovery connecting our culturally rich and diverse community to resources and services that promote lifelong learning, personal growth and development, and awareness of the arts."

Consider the mission and vision of your library as you develop programs to advance and deepen the learning of tweens and teens. Students can take advantage of what the library has to offer and search the collections and online resources to obtain the answers to their questions, thereby advancing and deepening their learning. They can then go into the community to further their knowledge.

Now that you know it is important to define exactly what programming means, it's time to ask why programming is critical for you and in your library, and to establish ideas for goals you wish to achieve through library programs.

Start with the Why

In many sectors, a key concept in professional development is finding your why. Simon Sinek's TED Talk "Start with Why," and his 2017 book *Finding Your Why* helped to popularize this concept (TEDx Talks, 2009). Everyone will have a different why depending on the campus or type of library you work in and the patrons you serve. During the 2019–2020 school year, librarians in the school district where Valerie works were asked, "What is your why? Why are you doing what you do, and how do you do it?"

What does finding your why mean, and why is it important? It is a reflection on the purpose of your work as a librarian and the outcomes you desire to see as a result of this work. Change is a constant in any profession, particularly professions that are rooted in service to the community. Libraries are no different, as they operate within or alongside many sectors: K–12 and higher education, city or county governments, health care, and more. No matter what type of library you serve in, it is important to take a step back and reflect on the purpose of library work and library programming.

Start this exploration by asking the following questions. In your answers, you may discover things about yourself that will help guide you in your path and help you develop a clear set of goals.

Questions to Help Define Your Why

Reflection questions such as "Why are you doing what you do?" may also include:

- Why did you become a librarian, and what are the professional goals you set for yourself to achieve?
- What is the essence of your work?
- What motivates you to do the work you are doing in the library?
- Who is the community you serve, and what are their information needs, educational needs, personal needs, and goals?

Similar questions can be applied to library programming:

- Why is programming critical in your library?
- What results do you want to achieve as a result of library programming?

Additional key points for reflection are:

- What brings students or patrons to the library?
- Did a program or event further their learning?
- What made it such a positive experience that they returned to the library?

To take the reflection further, examine why programs are held in the library:

- Are programs just to mark an occasion, such as a change in month and season?
- Is the reason for organizing programs curriculum-driven?
- Is a particular program the trend in libraries, in vogue at the time? That is, are programs created due to a current event or current trends, such as a new film?

The answers, of course, will vary depending upon the type of library and the population it serves. Curriculum instructional needs; student/patron interests; community interests and needs; technology, its availability, or even lack of; and funding all have an impact on library programs.

After reflection, seek out a framework from which to build programming upon, such as the ISTE Standards.

Standards and Library Programming

Standards can serve as a framework or a basis for library programming. In school state curriculum standards—for example, the Texas Essential Knowledge and Skills (TEKS) or the Common Core Standards that are used in various states throughout the country—are the basis of instruction. Curriculum standards basically state what educators should teach students at each grade level. The standards can also be tied to library programming. In schools where librarians are required to create lesson plans that include what state standards are covered, librarians can also tie standards to library programs and events.

In writing a lesson plan for library programs, create a SMART (Specific, Measurable, Achievable, Relevant, and Time-Bound) goal for programs that incorporate the standards, stating what the students and patrons have learned or what they will be able to do after attending the program. Public librarians can do the same in collaboration with school librarians and incorporate state curriculum standards and national standards from professional organizations such as ISTE, American Association of School Librarians (AASL), Future Ready, or Association of College & Research Libraries (ACRL), depending on the type of library and the patrons served.

AASL Reading Standards

 Explore the AASL Standards and related resources. (standards.aasl.org)

The American Association of School Librarians (AASL) has developed some standards for school libraries to adhere to when designing programming. These can be helpful in thinking about your programming and to advocate for your goals in terms of the standards.

For example:

Inquire. How will programming support students' learning to inquire about their world through fiction and nonfiction?

Include. What efforts does library programming make to include students and community members from historically marginalized or disenfranchised groups (for example, special education, English language learners, or visually impaired students)?

Collaborate. How do students collaborate with one another in library spaces (for example, creating digital book reviews)?

Curate. How are students included in the process of curation?

Explore. What library programs encourage students to explore the world outside the physical or virtual library space (for example, collaborating with local museums and organizations offering programs for young people)?

Engage. How are young people engaging others in the world around them through sharing their experiences in the library (for example, community book clubs or whole-school reading initiatives)?

ISTE Standards for Educators

 Explore the ISTE Standards and related resources. (iste.org/standards)

The ISTE Standards for Educators can be used by librarians as a framework to develop effective and successful programs for all types of libraries that serve teens and young adults. The shift to online programming that libraries were forced to make due to the COVID-19 pandemic proved to be a challenge to some librarians. The need to innovate and become tech savvy in a short amount of time definitely presented a challenge. However, many were able to make the transition and build on their technology integration skills by earning certifications and participating in tech webinars during this time. It has never been more important to the future of library programming and library services to integrate technology and innovation in programming instruction for the digital realm than it is now.

The following ISTE Standards in particular stand out for programming from the librarian's perspective.

ISTE Standards for Educators

2.3.b. Establish a learning culture that promotes curiosity and critical examination of online resources and fosters digital literacy and media fluency.

2.4a. Dedicate planning time to collaborate with colleagues to create authentic learning experiences that leverage technology.

2.4.b. Collaborate and co-learn with students to discover and use new digital resources and diagnose and troubleshoot technology issues.

2.4.c. Use collaborative tools to expand students' authentic, real-world learning experiences by engaging virtually with experts, teams, and students, locally and globally.

2.5.a. Use technology to create, adapt, and personalize learning experiences that foster independent learning and accommodate learner differences and needs.

2.6.a. Foster a culture where students take ownership of their learning goals and outcomes in both independent and group settings.

2.6.c. Create learning opportunities that challenge students to use a design process and computational thinking to innovate and solve problems.

ISTE AASL and Future Ready Librarians Crosswalks

 See the National School Library Standards crosswalk with ISTE Standards. (bit.ly/3ixxyV7)

In order to utilize the ISTE Standards into programming and other activities surrounding programming such as program promotion, collaboration with other educators, and measuring programming results, librarians can refer to the ISTE Standards crosswalks that are available from AASL and Future Ready Librarians. The crosswalks help librarians look at how their daily practices align with the Standards and see opportunities where they can grow and institute new practices and methods. School librarians can reference the crosswalk of AASL Standards and ISTE Standards for Students and Educators to ensure they are not only developing programming that allows learners to inquire, include, collaborate, curate, explore, and engage but also embed digital citizenship. Take the ISTE Standards further to help build out library programs.

Leverage the ISTE Standards and crosswalks in your program planning, be it in-person programming or online, program execution, and in assessment of the results of a program. Use them in developing yearly program goals. Leverage the standards and crosswalks in library reports to stakeholders in order to demonstrate the effect or impact Standards integration and implementation have on the purpose and power of library programming.

Many times, in order to fund programs, librarians (especially in the K–12 world) have to be grant writers. This is a perfect opportunity to leverage the ISTE Standards and crosswalks to tell the story of why the funds will be used, who the funds will be used for, and the sustainability of the programs.

Programming is multifaceted. Its basis may come out of the personal and professional goals librarians wish to achieve or its framework, or justification may lie in the Standards. It can be based on student interests, community interests and needs, as well as curricular/instructional needs, but it must also fit into library budgets and be scheduled at optimum times. This leads us to scheduling and time—not just time to hold programs but the time to develop them and curate resources and supplies for them, along with the technology and tools that will be used and more.

Who Has the Time?

Scheduling is a component of educational spaces that both fascinates and perplexes librarians. Julia has always been interested in the mystery of the process that is the "Master Schedule," finding it fascinating that so many moving parts and pieces come together in a way that works for hundreds, sometimes thousands of people. However, these days, living and writing these words in the time of a global pandemic, she has observed that scheduling has become a new sort of challenge, as administrators and educators become accustomed to the work and language of "cohorts" and "cross-contamination."

Scheduling has to be communicated more as a suggestion than an absolutely hard-and-fast rule everyone must follow. As educators, we know that a schedule is only as effective as those who adhere to it are able to be dedicated. Though scheduling in library spaces sometimes has more flexibility than the scheduling of a traditional classroom teacher, librarians can and do still design time in a way that supports the achievement of both long- and short-term goals.

One example is monthly recurring library appointments with individual classes. Educators set up the recurring library visit appointments during the first beginning-of-the-school-year orientation, then choose from a menu of options provided by the librarian for subsequent calendar appointments. Some offerings might include "Critical Media Literacy" or "Independent Reading Support."

Online and Hybrid Programming

As of the year of publication for this book, library programs during the pandemic have had to be creative about programming as part of the continuing work of advocating for librarian positions, which continue to be eliminated at an astonishing rate, and as the work of adapting to the needs of learning communities shifts between in-person, hybrid, and completely virtual forms, sometimes overnight. Though for so many of us, the constantly changing amounts of time we actually have with students has been a challenge, for some students, the flexibility of hybrid and virtual learning environments allows freedom to access libraries and learning in ways that simply were not commonplace before. Nontraditional students and those who benefit from a more flexible, home-based learning environment have flourished during this time. It's safe to say that the way we schedule educational programs has changed forever.

For the purposes of librarianship, we have begun to envision a new era with almost limitless time to engage young people with the act of reading and all the joys experienced when people come together around the stories that unite us.

Making Time

Librarians are pressed for time. Calendars are booked with classes, and school librarians are often looking to carve out time to collaborate with staff by attending professional learning community meetings with teachers on campuses and with other librarians. It may be helpful to have an overarching plan of programming for the year. Utilize the calendar for your institution and sketch out a plan months or a year in advance. Set deadlines, gather input and ideas, review results and reports from the previous year, then forge ahead with the programming plan.

Along with the changes that have happened to educational programming as a whole, the role of the librarian shifted and adapted to fit virtual, hybrid, and in-person spaces during the COVID-19 pandemic. A common misconception is that the only, or primary, role of the librarian is circulating physical books. Librarians are not only the principal architects of school-wide reading culture; we are also responsible for developing independent reading programs and supporting them, managing collections, monitoring circulation, and developing support for community engagement. All of these initiatives require a level of advocacy and collaboration to develop and maintain.

For Julia, she knows that her time as a librarian looks very different from the way her time was organized as a classroom teacher. She no longer has specific periods during which she has to be engaged in certain tasks. She no longer has prep periods to take care of the "business" of education, including grading and entering grades into a virtual platform. She does spend hours and hours, if not days, preparing spreadsheets of titles for a virtual order form for our free book fair. She has also done an inventory that took weeks and weeks, full days of scanning titles, and participated in a genrefication process that took five people over a week and a half to complete. So when designing library programming, an important part of her process is to consider both long- and short-term projects that need to be completed in order to keep the library running smoothly, as well as programming she would like to recur every year in order to gain momentum and establish a sense of tradition.

Reimagining Library Legacies

In popular media, librarians are often stereotypically depicted as female, bespectacled, and aggressively defending the sanctity of a silent environment. As more and more libraries adapt to become spaces that live virtually, as well as in physical spaces, it seems like an excellent time to reframe what it means to be a librarian and reenvision some of the images that are pervasive within society. When creating a plan for programming, think about each student's individual experience as part of the story of our collective experience. What is it like to be a part of our library community during the time spent in the school system? What is the legacy you would like to leave behind? Furthermore, what will students think about their experiences with the library when they go on to the next level of their education—and many years after, when they look back as adults?

WE DO THIS IN COMMUNITY
Protecting Students' Rights to Read

Since her time as a full-time classroom teacher, Julia no longer thinks in terms of a year-long plan, especially after this past year spent teaching during a pandemic. Flexibility is so important when designing library programming, and making time for lane changes along the road to where you want to be is crucial. Another point of consideration is, as activist and organizer Mariame Kaba says in an interview for *Adi Magazine*, "Everything worthwhile is done with other people" (Ewing, 2019). Though reading is thought of as a solitary activity, so much of what we do in library spaces can and should be done in community. When we work together to build a reading community, we dismantle the stereotypical depiction of an authoritarian librarian enforcing rules and regulations, making the library a place where few patrons feel welcome.

One of the most important actions Julia takes at the beginning of each year is to survey students first, then staff, so she can see what kinds of programming they liked from the year before and what their attitudes about, and experiences with, reading have been. She then uses the data from the surveys to design programming, with several check-ins along the way. For example, if students have stated they don't read much of their assigned reading, but enjoy graphic novels and manga, Julia might develop a plan to work with language arts teachers to support curriculum development around popular graphic novels or manga.

Though it takes time to get new content for courses approved, students can often be wonderful advocates for the types of reading they like to do. Making time for students to build a community around the books they like to read and with people who share their interests is essential. World-renowned educator and reading advocate Donalynn Miller has said,

> Students will read if we give them the books, the time, and the enthusiastic encouragement to do so. If we make them wait for the one unit a year in which they are allowed to choose their own books and become readers, they may never read at all. To keep our students reading, we have to let them. (2009)

Unfortunately, independent reading is often an activity that commonly gets the least amount of support, particularly in environments that prioritize high-stakes testing. In all environments, but particularly those with high populations of students belonging to groups that have been historically disenfranchised or marginalized, it is the work of whole communities, not just individual librarians and literacy advocates, to come together to protect a student's right to read—and the time to do so.

In 2019, the International Literacy Association created a document defending children's rights to read (see Figure 1.1). The document and accompanying position statement states, "Children have the right to extended time set aside for reading." In a time when virtual learning is becoming more normalized, it is crucial for librarians to learn about what "extended time ...

for reading" means in their specific learning environments and to design programming accordingly. This may include reading initiatives that are more flexible with time and space, and that do not happen during traditional school hours, but live in a virtual space so students and the larger community can access the content at times that are convenient for them. Historically, educational, non-profit, and public institutions focus reading initiatives on defining and defending reading time for our youngest students, but all students, at all levels, need and deserve to have their reading lives nurtured and time for reading defended.

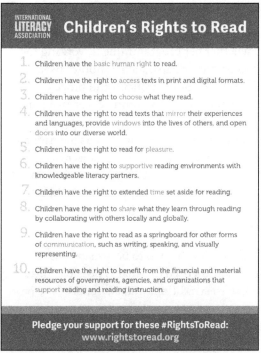

Figure 1.1 "Children's Rights to Read" by International Literacy Association. Download the poster at bit.ly/3KSy5Nv.

How to Tell What Programs Are Right for Your School Culture

Library programs should be as unique as the communities they serve. However, it is helpful to consider some basic points of organization, which we will discuss further in Chapter 5. When organizing her library program for the year, Julia breaks it into three components:

- actions I could take as a librarian,

- actions teachers and administrators can do to support, and

- what students can do to participate.

She regularly collects data via surveys and informal conversations to understand whether her programming is working for all stakeholders and to better see gaps, such as library users who are privileged or excluded by her policies and procedures. Each stakeholder in an educational community has different demands on their time, so when developing the ideal program, it's important to recognize time constraints, but as mentioned previously, remain flexible and expansive with respect to envisioning what is possible. At every step, it's important to help library patrons (and those in charge of supporting the library) see what is possible within the world of education technology because so much is changing so fast.

As a librarian, Julia believes it is her job to be a visionary, to remain curious, and to stay focused on what is possible, rather than remaining stuck in the traditions and customs of the past.

LIBRARIAN SPOTLIGHT

Bethany Dietrich, Public Services Librarian
at Bastrop Public Library in Bastrop, Texas

The best thing I have done to promote a strong, positive culture in my library is to encourage my teen patrons to bring their own ideas for weekly programs and coach them on what we need to do to adjust their ideas to fit our 90-minute time slot, very small budget, and safety concerns. This practice took time because I had to really listen to their ideas; brainstorm out loud the modifications to make it safe, cheap, and time-appropriate; and convey all that back while sharing how I loved their original idea. It has really been about building their confidence that their ideas are valid (with some tweaking) and that I value their opinions. I started doing this in winter 2018, and it took at least six months for them to feel comfortable just walking up to me or emailing me their ideas and modification "plans."

If other librarians were to replicate this practice, I recommend starting by making sure that your teens know (and believe) that you truly care about their likes and dislikes. You can do this by having people share YouTube videos the first (or last) 15 minutes of the program (set some guidelines, of course, so that you aren't blasting curse words through the projector speakers).

Next, make sure you're already planning programs that 1) may not go as planned (Failure is okay! Model for them what it looks like when you fail and how you should respond to failure.) and 2) aren't "typical" library programs. Let them run around, and don't make everything book or curriculum-centric. Maybe play ultimate frisbee one week, do messy relays, play human foosball, or carve bars of soap.

In all, this approach allows us to celebrate when someone's program idea is a lot of fun. It also allows us to try new things we wouldn't necessarily think of trying. Lastly, it builds patrons' self-confidence, showing that their ideas—and therefore they themselves—are valid.

———————————○———————————

Be Flexible

In Marlon Carey's 2012 TED Talk "About Time," the slam poet ruminates about the nature of our clockwork existence, and the saying, "We all have the same twenty-four hours in a day." Library life, though, has changed dramatically in the way that we, as librarians, organize our time. Simultaneously, the times and formats in which patrons can access the items we have in our collections have also transformed.

If we think of libraries like a Rubik's cube, instead of a flat square, they are now so much more than just a quiet place for people to come and escape from the world. Library time can happen anywhere and anytime, with virtual libraries, ebooks, and audiobook collections accessible 24/7 on any number of devices. The time it used to take to read books is also different now that we have the ability to read graphic novels and comics on e-readers, zooming in to see detail and taking time to click on embedded external links. Audiobooks can be read at 1.25 speed, enabling readers to listen to favorite books faster while multitasking or commuting to school or work, for example. Librarians and the tools that help us are also available anytime, now that search algorithms are smart enough to learn an end user's preferences and make book recommendations that match as soon as a title is completed.

A Change in Plans

If the year 2020 taught us anything, it is that plans change. However, librarians are flexible and creative. If the budget, equipment, technical capacity, and pure ingenuity are available, programming can be done virtually or in a hybrid environment. In Valerie's experience at a public library, the go-to word to describe a change in plans or a shift during this period has been "pivot." Librarians must have a pivot plan. If conditions determine that a shift or change to how a program is presented must be done, can you pivot? Can you join forces with other staff and departments or librarians at other schools or cities to present programs in the event of a sudden change?

Key Points

So now that we have the tools and technology to maximize time in the library and access to it, how does all of this come together? It's about time we rework the time we have and reimagine what can happen in library spaces.

- Libraries can now exist in virtual and physical places simultaneously, so librarians do not have to limit library time to what happens during traditional school hours. Some activities that can happen anytime include virtual author visits, community book club conversations, collaborating via digital book reviews, and/or blending the worlds between curriculum and independent reading.

- Consider both long- and short-term goals and develop library programming that explicitly connects to library advocacy. Focus attention on how libraries can support individual, school, community, and curricular objectives.

- We have come a long way from the stereotypical library space where information gatekeepers keep patrons from accessing the collection and one another with the stereotypical "Shhhhh!" followed by a hard stare.

- We all need to work in community to make sure a legacy lasts, because the work is so much bigger than any one individual.

- Though the age of technology and information continues to surprise us with tools that help librarians maximize time spent on the work of librarianship, we each still have the same twenty-four hours in a day. Modifying thinking about what is possible and, even more importantly, when library time can happen, benefits everyone.

Reflection

- What do you want your community to take away from their library experience, and how will your organization of time reflect that?

- Do you have a plan in place to make a shift in programming, if needed?

- What technology tools do you currently have, and do they have the capacity to help deliver programming if a pivot or shift must be made?

- What do you want your legacy to be as a librarian?

- How do you currently engage with the community in terms of programming and working to serve tweens and teens?

CHAPTER 2

Everyone Is Welcome

For library programming to be successful, tweens and teens must feel comfortable coming to the library. They should know they are welcome to visit, especially at times in the day when they can elect to be elsewhere. For example, in a school library some programs can be held before school, during lunch, and after school—which are usually times school libraries host events that are not tied to instruction. At public libraries, teens typically visit in the evenings and on the weekend. Homeschooled teens and families may visit in the daytime. Many public libraries have dedicated teen spaces, where visitors can browse print collections, use computers, or occupy designated seating spaces for leisure reading or to study and work on assignments and projects. Teen spaces also serve as the dedicated place and space for teen programs. Colleges and universities have large facilities and the capacity to host a variety of programs to serve students at various times of the day.

A Philosophy for Creating a Welcoming Environment

Welcoming students to the library and making them feel like it is a place and space where they can be comfortable—working, studying, and participating in programs—is the overarching goal in ensuring that everyone is welcome. Valerie calls it "Akwaaba librarianship." "Akwaaba" means welcome in Twi, a language spoken in Ghana. When you deplane a flight at Kotoka International Airport in Accra, one of the first words you will see is "Akwaaba" above the doors of the terminal. Welcoming others is an integral part of Ghanaian life that Valerie has grown up with, as her parents are from Ghana. She makes an effort to bring that aspect of her culture into her work as a librarian.

There are too many stories of libraries where teens aren't always welcome, even in school libraries. It is time to change the narrative. You can start by evaluating how teens are welcomed to the library and how they feel about library services like programming.

Student Agency

In addition to a welcoming environment, student involvement and student voice (or agency) are also important to programming success. When students have a sense of ownership, they are more likely to attend and participate in programs and get more involved in the library. One way to bring about ownership or student agency is to sponsor a club or group and elect tween and teen officers. The officers can meet with library staff to provide valuable insight and ideas for programming, collection development, instruction, fundraising, and even library operations. Frequent visitors to public libraries, or teens who public libraries interface with on a regular basis, can provide that needed voice or input.

Evaluating How Tweens and Teens Experience the Library

Public Libraries

- Are tweens and teens provided with customer service? Are they welcomed and greeted when they visit the library?
- Does the library provide a variety of tween- and teen-specific services and programming?
- What engagement have you had with tweens and teens?
- How can library staff further develop relationships with tweens and teens to ensure they feel welcomed in the library and take part in library programs and initiatives?

School Libraries

- Are all students welcomed into the school library, regardless of literacy proficiency, and are they comfortable there?
- What changes need to be made to the physical space to ensure students' needs are met?
- How do school librarians engage with students? Are students comfortable with speaking with librarians and sharing information needs and programming ideas with them?

Librarians and educators can keep a pulse on patron interests and needs through working with various groups in the community, and this will also assist in gaining input from teens who may not visit libraries on a regular basis.

In Texas, where Valerie works, many cities have a Mayor's Teen Council, a program of the Texas Municipal League. Public and school librarians can tap this council as a focus group to get information and bridge the information gaps that may exist for teens in the community. This may be an excellent group that public librarians can gain insight from as far as programming and services, and even have the teens volunteer at library events.

LIBRARIAN SPOTLIGHT

Daniela Lankford, Librarian at Klein Oak High School in Spring, Texas

I partner with the art teachers on my campus to have an art show every spring. It's called Books Love Art. We set up the library like a museum, ask orchestra students to provide musical entertainment, and serve light refreshments. The show is up for a week, but one evening it is open to the community so parents and anyone else can come. The students whose artwork is shown have individual invitations for their teachers that they hand deliver. Administrators, board members, and central office personnel are always invited, and our superintendent attends every year. The artwork is identified with artist name, grade level and class name, teacher's name, and any awards or scholarships they may have earned. The artists hang out around their work to discuss with anyone interested. It's a wonderful evening.

A Space for Building Community

When we think about the school library as a place where reading communities begin and are nurtured, we have to remember that a school is a place where many students do not inherently feel welcome. Historically speaking, school systems have been an instrumental part of systems of colonization and indoctrination. In Ngũgĩ wa Thiong'o's famous essay "Decolonising the Mind" (1986), we learn that students have been socialized to shame one another for speaking Kikuyu, their mother tongue. The tendency to demonize the unique parts of us that make us individuals, and to praise or reward the parts of people that demonstrate their assimilation with the dominant culture is pervasive throughout all of humankind. From Japan, which kept its borders closed to visitors from the West (until the arrival of Commodore Perry in 1853), all the way to the Hawaiian Islands, whose indigenous population was decimated with the arrival of colonizers and smallpox in 1778, education has been used to dominate and subjugate throughout human history.

So what can we do to transform our educational system from one of subjugation and assimilation to one where everyone is truly welcome, a system based upon precepts of liberation and freedom?

Culturally Relevant Librarianship

The idea of culturally relevant librarianship is a natural outgrowth of culturally responsive education. Many have written and taught about culturally relevant pedagogy, or CRP (not to be confused with CRT) and it is the child of what began as multicultural education. When we think about culturally relevant librarianship, we have to consider that librarianship is in essence the curation, preservation, and dissemination of information and story. We must also remember that historically, information and stories have been the record of those who considered themselves to be the winners, the conquerors in societies the world over.

In modern times, what we call CRP was coined by Gloria Ladson-Billings as a way in which we remain responsive to and aware of the need of all children to have an experience (in library and classroom environments) that is empowering, restorative, and validating.

As you begin to explore culturally responsive librarianship, begin by asking yourself the following:

How do we make sure students feel empowered? We lift up stories and information that depict all people, not just those of the global majority, as inventors, explorers, discoverers, and victors.

How do we make sure students are restored through the information they seek and find? We make sure information seeking is a collaborative process and one that includes search terms, keywords, and databases that center around people and funds of knowledge outside those of Western Europe.

How do we validate students in an effort to make sure they truly feel welcome in library space? We center their funds of knowledge and make sure they know their stories are valued and valid, even if those from the dominant culture do not understand the cultural norms, language, and value depicted within them.

Developing Cultural Competency

Understanding and undertaking this work is a process. According to Monteil-Overall and Reyes-Escudero (2015, p. 24), a continuum of cultural competency exists, from cultural incapacity to cultural proficiency:

Cultural incapacity. Failure to understand why a person would need to understand anyone else's culture.

Cultural blindness. Individuals claim not to see differences between individuals and feel it is inappropriate to discuss differences.

Cultural awareness. Individuals candidly recognize differences and have some knowledge of what makes individuals ethnically, racially, linguistically, culturally, or in other ways unique.

Cultural competence. Individuals who adapt their practice to meet the needs of those around them.

Cultural proficiency. Individuals with the capacity to understand social justice issues and who work to eliminate inequities faced by cultural groups. (Adapted from Mardis & Oberg, 2019.)

In order to support people of any age moving along the continuum, it is important to seek tools that facilitate conversation, to read and study them, and to do the internal work of interrogating our own biases and how they have been formed. For example:

 Librarians curating collections can look to socialjusticebooks.org for examples of book lists or readers' advisory suggestions that align with specific cultural/ethnic/racial groups.

 Librarians looking to develop their understanding of how library classification systems may be exclusionary or biased may read this *Smithsonian* article: bit.ly/36eAcMx

 Librarians looking to depart from the Western methods of library classification may choose to organize library materials with an indigenous system of knowledge classification, like this example from the University of British Columbia: bit.ly/3KEpVI6

Many librarians have chosen to genrefy their libraries in an attempt to emulate the organization systems used by bookstores. Genrefication is a step toward student empowerment and away from dependence. Learn more from this article in *American Libraries* magazine: bit.ly/3vZiFTp

Figure 2.1 One guide to CRP that provides a framework for readers to follow is Lorena Germán's *Textured Teaching: A Framework for Culturally Sustaining Pracitces.*

Readings on Culturally Relevant Librarianship

What would a book for librarians be without a wealth of reading recommendations? Fortunately, the field is rich with resources to help create more welcoming, culturally relevant educational spaces. The following books are ideal for study or as part of a book study with colleagues.

Social Justice and Cultural Competency: Essential Readings for School Librarians, edited by Marcia A. Mardis and Dianne Oberg (bit.ly/3ubvV4R). This essay collection features approaches to dealing with research and evidence-based best practices pertaining to cultural competency in the work of librarianship and ways to anchor librarianship in key components of social justice.

Let's Talk: Facilitating Critical Conversations with Students (bit.ly/3N0Kd0E) Learning for Justice (formerly Teaching Tolerance) has provided this handbook to facilitate critical conversations in classrooms and other educational settings.

Not Light, But Fire: How to Lead Meaningful Race Conversations in the Classroom by Matthew R. Kay (stenhouse.com/content/not-light-fire) Matthew R. Kay contributes practical and actionable advice for those looking to lead critical conversations about race in the classroom (or libraries). Matthew is a current classroom educator, and well-respected voice in the field of education.

This Book Is Anti-Racist: 20 Lessons on How to Wake Up, Take Action and Do the Work by Tiffany Jewell, with illustrations by Aurélia Durand (bit. ly/362jd0h) Tiffany Jewell provides tools for self-reflection and community conversations about developing an anti-racist stance through twenty lessons about anti-racism. The book also provides background information about racism, how many societies contain undercurrents of racism that work their way into all aspects of human interaction, and how we can begin to unify in order to heal.

Courageous Conversations About Race, Third Edition: A Field Guide for Achieving Equity in Schools and Beyond by Glenn E. Singleton (bit.ly/36pFIMg) Both a book, workbook, and course, this guide offers opportunities for those in organizational leadership to challenge their policies and practices through a process that begins with meaningful conversation.

Resources for Connecting Curriculum and Culturally Relevant Pedagogy

Free Within Ourselves: The Development of African American Children's Literature by Rudine Sims Bishop (bit.ly/3MTxlns)

Asian Americans in Story: Context, Collections, and Community Engagement with Children's and Young Adult Literature by Sarah Park Dahlen and Paul Lai (alastore.ala.org/aastory)

An Indigenous Peoples' History of the United States by Roxanne Dunbar-Ortiz (bit.ly/3qeyim9)

Culturally Relevant Pedagogy: Asking a Different Question by Gloria Ladson-Billings (bit.ly/3Jo8Ba6)

Indigenous and Decolonizing Studies in Education: Mapping the Long View, edited by Linda Tuhiwai Smith (bit.ly/3uahE8g)

Culturally Sustaining Pedagogies: Teaching and Learning for Justice in a Changing World by Django Paris and H. Samy Alim (bit.ly/3qdVvok)

Decolonizing Methodologies: Research and Indigenous Peoples by Linda Tuhiwai Smith (bit.ly/3uaQvSy)

The Dark Fantastic: Race and the Imagination from Harry Potter to the Hunger Games by Ebony Elizabeth Thomas (bit.ly/3CTK3TX)

Textured Teaching: A Framework for Culturally Sustaining Practices by Lorena Escoto Germán (bit.ly/3wmFP6p)

LIBRARIAN SPOTLIGHT

Nancy Jo Lambert, Librarian at Reedy High School in Frisco, Texas

In the 2019–2020 school year, and again in the 2020–2021 school year, librarian Nancy Jo Lambert implemented a Staff Diversity Reading Challenge, which was voluntary and shared with all staff. Through this challenge, she created professional development to build cultural competence through reading diverse books.

The National Education Association defines cultural competency as "having an awareness of one's own cultural identity and views about difference, and the ability to learn and build on the varying cultural and community norms of students and their families. It is the ability to understand the within-group differences that make each student unique, while celebrating the between-group variations that make our country a tapestry." Leading educators suggest cultural competence can: help close the achievement gap, reduce discipline referrals, and improve student outcomes.

At the time of the challenge, the demographics at Lambert's school were:

- Hispanic: 11.22%

- Native American/Alaskan Native: 0.67%

- Asian: 28.75%

- Black: 6.88%

- Native Hawaiian/Pacific Islander: 0.00%

- White: 48.60%

- Two or more: 3.88%

Being culturally competent means that educators are prepared to acknowledge how a student's culture impacts their daily life and activities both inside and outside the classroom. It also means that educators are familiar with how a student's culture influences their communication practices and enables the educator to better communicate with students and families.

For the challenge, staff was required to read at least one book from a list that included *The Hate U Give, Indigenous History of the United States for Young People, I Am Not Your Perfect Mexican Daughter,* and others. Participants were encouraged to read books over breaks and all through the school year. For each book they read, they wrote a response to these prompts:

1. How is this relevant to my teaching practice?

2. How can I use what I learned to improve my relationships with students from marginalized communities?

See the full presentation for the challenge, including the book titles, here: bit.ly/RHSRead20

Library Skills for a Lifetime

When everyone is working to develop skills for a lifetime, we must make sure students understand the skills they are cultivating in library spaces will be useful to them beyond their time in the formalized education system. Helping students understand what it means to exercise their full participatory citizenship is a key component of school librarianship. But what does it mean to live in a democratic society when we are not all treated as equal?

In her autobiography, *Living for Change*, Grace Lee Boggs states,

The oppressed internalize the values of the oppressor. Therefore, any group that achieves power, no matter how oppressed, is not going to act differently from their oppressors as long as they have not confronted the values that they have internalized and consciously adopted different values. (1998, pp. 151–152)

For Julia, as someone in a position of leadership—as a leader of educators and librarians—she has a responsibility to make sure that those who are oppressed and those who are in a position to oppress others understand their values, rights, and responsibilities to themselves and others. As an individual who has lived and experienced the several intersections of interpersonal and institutional oppression, she feels a responsibility to make sure she protects and improves conditions for those who may be having the same or a similar experience.

When we design a curriculum, we have to keep in mind that all curriculum is an extension of the great arm of colonization, and we must remember that the students themselves are not empty vessels. They come to us with knowledge and cultural competency, many literacies that develop from navigating the world, their family relationships, and extended communities. We have a professional and social obligation to acknowledge and uplift student "funds of knowledge" (Amanti, Gonzalez, et al., 2001) if we intend for practices of reading and learning to continue beyond the commodified and extrinsically rewarded school systems we develop and maintain. Learning does not happen in a vacuum, and the young people who come to libraries and classrooms are not in possession of minds or souls that are vacant before we, their educators, arrive. So how do we go about acknowledging the funds of knowledge our students bring? How do we validate them and, at the same time, spark curiosity about the wider world that exists beyond the realm of their experience?

LIBRARIAN SPOTLIGHT

*Stephanie Singer, Library Media Specialist at
Readington Middle School in Bridgewater, New Jersey*

I started the Junior Librarians program at my middle school and
it has consistently grown over the years across all three grades.
One year we had twenty-nine participants. My Junior Librarians
are enthusiastic helpers and have a profound sense of ownership
of the Library Media Center. Whenever possible, we meet during
the students' Academic Support classes. They receive training in
shelving, circulation, book processing, and marketing to create
book displays. Junior Librarians has expanded to include an
afterschool club that meets once or twice a month on Monday
afternoons. During these meetings we tackle larger projects like
updating our monthly hallway bulletin boards or genrefying our
nonfiction section.

We have conducted two field trips: one to Princeton Public
Library and Firestone Library at Princeton University, and
the other to Alexander Library at Rutgers University and the
Gardner A. Sage Library in New Brunswick, New Jersey. We were
given private tours of the facilities in order to see how public
and academic libraries function. At each venue, the staff were
impressed with the number of participants we had and their
interest in libraries and reading. The students enjoyed the experiences and we hope to initiate another field trip.

I recognize exemplary behavior and effort with the Junior
Librarian of the Month award. Junior Librarians approach me
asking how they can earn the award. I consistently have students
who enthusiastically identify as a Junior Librarian. Their level of
commitment and alacrity are a constant source of joy for me.

WE DO THIS IN COMMUNITY
Creating Understanding and Connection with "Others" in the Community

Educator and community organizer bell hooks said, "As a classroom community, our capacity to generate excitement is deeply affected by our interest in one another, in hearing one another's voices, in recognizing one another's presence" (1994). We know that learners are more likely to read and sustain interest in books they are interested in and can make personal connections to. How can we make connections to stories that are distant from our lived experiences? One of the ways we do this is by looking for titles that explore imagined worlds and those that find areas of synchronicity between the lives of characters and the events of the real world. This is part of the reason so many of the books that are the most popular with young people today have aspects of commentary about the real world or are imagined retellings of actual historical events.

However, at the time of this book's publication there is much discussion about whose lived experiences are "school appropriate" and which stories and discussions belong in school. It is perhaps more imperative now than ever for educators to involve communities in the reading of and discussion about texts in our schools. Some ways to do this include:

- Writing letters to families at the beginning of the year that detail the texts that will be read for the year and include a short philosophy about why educators may believe a particular text is worthy of academic study.

- Collecting student anecdotes and book reviews in various formats (podcast episodes, written anecdotal responses, sound clips, and short videos).

- Inviting community members and stakeholders to take part in whole-school read-ins once or twice a year that highlight certain books that have been banned.

- Collecting student achievement data pre- and post-reading specific titles.

As previously mentioned, many associations have released statements defending the right to read. Here are a few more examples.

 Texas Library Association statement on defending the right to read (bit.ly/3Jq9Bun)

 NCTE Statement on Independent Reading (bit.ly/3qhcwy7)

Mapping the "Other"

The adjacent "other" are groups that individuals self-identify as close to the self. In the case of an African American female, an adjacent other might be a Latina female who might also experience colorism and sexism. The distant "other" might be an Asian male or white male. It's important to recognize why we participate in "othering." The opposing action is creating spaces of belonging and inclusion. In her work *Teaching Community: A Pedagogy of Hope*, bell hooks wrote:

> Dominator culture has tried to keep us all afraid, to make us choose safety instead of risk, sameness instead of diversity. Moving through that fear, finding out what connects us, reveling in our differences—this is the process that brings us closer, that gives us a world of shared values, of meaningful community. (2003)

Use the following diagram to help those in your community unpack the various components of individual identity and why we connect with those whom we feel share our identity markers and lived experiences. It is often easier to connect with those who fall into the category of "adjacent other" simply because those feelings of fear are mitigated or absent entirely. However, when we do as bell hooks suggests and move through feelings of fear to find out what connects us, we can begin to build a meaningful, and what has often been termed "beloved," community (philosopher-theologian Josiah Royce and then popularized by Dr. Martin Luther King Jr.).

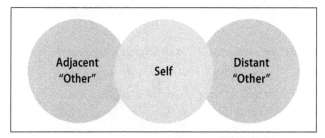

Figure 2.2 Venn diagram showing the self in relation to the adjacent and distant other.

You can also refer to the following resource from the Equity Collective.

 Equity Collaborative: Supporting Positive Racial Identity Development (bit.ly/3igxljx)

Be Flexible

If we purport to believe that students are an important part of the present and future of any community, we acknowledge that their experiences in learning spaces should be driven by their questions, curiosities, habits, and tastes. Effective school and library leaders prioritize student experience over adult agendas.

This happens when we ask students for their input about how the school experience is going for them and act accordingly to change practices that are not resulting in student enjoyment and skills development.

Conduct a Needs Assessment

Traditionally, educators give assessments to determine progress. Librarians often conduct what is called a needs assessment. Julia calls hers a reading habits inventory. In it, she asks questions like:

- How many books did you read independently last year (outside of those assigned for class)?

- Do you think reading for pleasure will be important for your life after (MS/HS)?

- Would you call yourself a "reader"?

- How often do you read outside of school?

- What form(s) of reading do you like the most?

You can see the full assessment by scanning the QR code or visiting the link below.

Reading Habits Inventory/Needs Assessment (bit.ly/3CTcscY). Property of Julia E. Torres. All rights reserved.

After the results of the needs assessment were gathered, Julia shared them with the educators in her school community to let them know that though approximately 80% of the surveyed students did not see themselves as readers, 80% believed that reading was an important skill and would be important for their lives after their formal education.

Sharing the results of the survey with students and adults in
the community allowed them to unite to form shared goals
for literacy across the curriculum, and it helped get community buy-in for programs like DEAR (Drop Everything and
Read) Fridays and #MontbelloReads one-book, one-school
programming. When attempting to get community buy-in, Julia
emphasized the importance of reading together as a communal
experience by taking students to see film *The Hate U Give* after
reading the book, about which students facilitated a lively and
thought-provoking discussion.

Be Prepared to Change Course

As with all school programs, it does take a measure of flexibility and willingness to change course if the journey demands
it. Though people often say it isn't good to "build the plane
while flying it," we also change direction when hiking if we find
ourselves at an undesirable or unknown destination, or when
we discover we've gotten lost. Similarly, though curriculum
maps and pacing guides are good, it is important to have a plan
and we must always remain flexible when feedback and student
experiences reveal that the intended course is not leading to the
desired destination. Remain flexible by regularly seeking feedback, making plans that are meant to expand as our knowledge
about what works changes and grows. Above all, we should
recognize that, as Mariame Kaba has stated, "Nothing that we
do that is worthwhile is done alone" (2010). Working in a team
requires flexibility, a willingness to be vulnerable and open to
receiving at the same time as we step into our strengths and
demonstrate a willingness to apply them to the service of others.
In order to do so, we have to address the ways we have been
socialized either to see, or not to see, strengths in ourselves and
others.

How to Create a Culturally Responsive Library Space

If we want our library spaces to be truly welcoming, they must be culturally responsive and inclusive. We must remember that historically, most educational spaces have prioritized and uplifted the forms of literacy that are of value to the dominant culture. It is crucial to become familiar with the language of oppression in order to deconstruct the systemic and interpersonal aspects that continue to do harm. Following are some social justice terms you may want to familiarize yourself with and add to your everyday vocabulary.

Social Justice Terms for Inclusive and Culturally Responsive Spaces

oppression	empathy	queer
power	appropriation	xenophobia
marginalization	gender binary	racism
erasure	gender expression	sexism
centering	intersectionality	colorism
allyship	prejudice	anti-Blackness
accomplice	privilege	

In library spaces, systems like the Dewey Decimal classification system have been deemed problematic and harmful. If we are truly committed to creating culturally responsive library spaces, it is our professional responsibility to learn about alternatives to such systems and to advocate for their system-wide adoption.

Racism in the Dewey Decimal System
(bit.ly/3lp355X)

Classification

Many librarians have chosen genrefication as one alternative to using traditional call-number systems for fiction collections. For nonfiction sections, some alternatives are the Universal Decimal Classification system, the BISAC Subject Codes, and the Library of Congress Classification system. One innovative approach to a classification system was developed by a rapper, activist, and self-proclaimed "hood librarian" who goes by the name "Noname." She created the Radical Hood Library in response to her community's need for a classification system that reflected their interests (Figure 2.3). Some examples of culturally responsive categories are "Black Radical Thought" and "Black Radical Resistance."

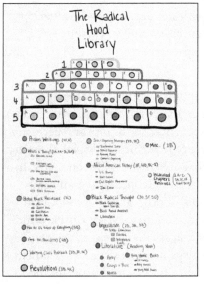

Figure 2.3 The Radical Hood Library classification system. Source: Noname Book Club (2021)

Another example of culturally responsive classification practices is the way one indigenous library chose to classify its materials. They adapted the Brian Deer system to develop and reflect the way indigenous people are very much alive today, rather than implying that native people, languages, and cultures belong to the past (Worth, 2019). In both instances, careful observation of the way users interacted with library spaces, programming, and materials revealed a need for the modification of existing systems.

Culturally Responsive Programming

Library programming centers around the reading of, experience with, and enjoyment of library materials. However, the experience that user groups have with library materials is not always the same. Various identity markers and lived experiences impact the way we experience school, and so they also influence the ways we experience and interact with the library. Ask yourself whether someone experiencing any specific set of intersecting identities is or could have the same enjoyment of the library space as an individual without those identities. Scorecards and evaluation tools like the ones shown in figures 2.4 and 2.5 can be useful when considering whether the spaces we create are truly inclusive for all learners.

Traditionally, library spaces center the dominant language. Community members and students are more likely to function independently in spaces that recognize the beauty and necessity of multilingualism as an aspect of living in a truly global society. This can look like programs that are occasionally conducted in a minoritized language with English-only speakers given head-phones and access to translation, or programming conducted exclusively in one of the many sign languages that exist around the world. Some other areas of marginalization (and intersectionality) are labels that identify gender identity and sexuality, the experience of living with or healing from adverse childhood experiences or trauma, and young people who may be neuro-diverse or hearing, vision, or speech impaired. The key is to decenter the historically and habitually centered and to bring to the front the experiences and voices of those forcibly relegated to the margins of society and history in ways that are consistent and sustainable.

Culturally Responsive Curriculum Scorecard

Representation

Diversity of Characters Tally

	Girl/Woman	Boy/Man	Non Binary	Total
Middle Eastern				
Asian/ Pacific Islander				
Black/ African				
Latinx				
Native American				
White				
Racially Ambiguous				
Multiracial				
People with Disabilities				
Animals				

Total # of characters depicted : _____

Figure 2.4 Culturally responsive scorecard for evaluating diversity of characters.

DIVERSITY OF AUTHORS

	Girl/Woman	Boy/Man	Non-Binary	TOTAL
Middle Eastern				
Asian/Pacific Islander				
Black/African				
Latinx				
Native American				
White				
Racially Ambiguous				
Multiracial				
People with Disabilities				

Figure 2.5 Scorecard for evaluating diversity of authors.

Diversity and Culturally Responsive Scorecards

 NYU Metro Center: Culturally Responsive-Sustaining STEAM Curriculum Scorecard (bit.ly/3wiHJVj)

 Teaching Tolerance: Reading Diversity Lite: A Tool for Selecting Diverse Texts (bit.ly/3KWI4Bq)

 Lee and Low Books: Classroom Library Questionnaire (bit.ly/36tK8Sa)

 Social Justice Books: Guide for Selecting Anti-Bias Children's Books (bit.ly/3wjOSoC)

Physical/Virtual Environment

Library physical environments have various components, such as signage, displays, shelving, and circulation areas. To serve the goals of cultural responsiveness and inclusivity, each of these must reflect the needs of various interest groups, as well as serve the dual purpose of providing information and sparking curiosity. Signage should be communicated in the dominant language, as well as in languages that belong to minoritized groups. Displays should include more than book covers, but reveal information about individuals and groups that showcase knowledge production in ways that will inspire young people to both make connections and remain curious.

For example, rather than a display for Indigenous Heritage Month with book covers by indigenous authors and stereotypical images of cultural items belonging to native peoples:

- Add titles by Native American authors to displays throughout the year, highlighting quotes and areas of intersectionality, such as Black-Indigenous people during Black History Month or on Juneteenth.

- Post QR codes that link to sound clips of Native American poets during National Poetry Month.

- Identify titles or short readings by indigenous people of the world (e.g., native Hawaiian or Central American people) to showcase all year long.

Kiara Garrett shared a suggested reading list, recommending books for those who liked a particular music album. The list, which was widely shared and liked on Facebook, includes artists Kendrick Lamar, Usher, and Solange Knowles, and books such as *Their Eyes Were Watching God* by Zora Neale Hurston, *The House on Mango Street* by Sandra Cisneros, and *Between the World and Me* by Ta-Nehisi Coates (see figure 2.6).

Figure 2.6 Example of a culturally responsive display.
Source: Kiara Garrett (2017)

Shelving and circulation areas should not only make all materials accessible, but showcase stories and information that students have communicated an interest in, as well as those they may not yet know about. Again, interest can be generated by drawing on the intersections between lived realities.

10 Tips for Creating a Culturally Responsive Library Space

1. Familiarize yourself with the language of decolonization.

2. Assess and evaluate materials and systems using a CRP scorecard and/or a collection audit scorecard.

3. Facilitate conversations in your community about steps to take.

4. Cocreate a library or classroom statement of purpose and beliefs.

5. Interrogate individual and systemic bias.

6. Read, study, and evaluate materials and programs for their cultural responsiveness and potential inclusion in your program.

7. Modify or develop new classification systems, programming, and additions to your physical environment.

8. Seek feedback from students about the effectiveness of efforts made.

9. Make adjustments and remain flexible.

10. Continue to study, interrogate, and evaluate the space you have created.

One must keep in mind the idea that culturally responsive library spaces have to continually evolve along with the population of library users and needs of the community. It is important to continually seek input from those who use the library (via various forms of needs assessments) to evaluate whether the library is in fact accessible by people of all cultures—not just the dominant one. It is also important to keep in mind that libraries, school libraries, and classroom libraries (even home libraries) must all function together as different pieces that create an individual's lifelong experience with literacy and help to form one's identity as a reader. This is detailed further as we discuss specific ways to build bridges between the K–12 library systems and those that serve the community of academics in higher education and beyond.

Perspectives from College Librarians

In addition to making libraries a welcoming place and space, it is important to craft programs that have students set sight on their future. Some will attend college after high school. Others are taking college classes right now and balancing high school, work, and other responsibilities, as well. School districts are shifting to offering early college, collegiate programs, and dual-credit courses to offer the opportunity to high-school students to earn an associate's degree and college credits while earning a high school diploma. This allows students to immediately go into the workforce or continue their education by earning a bachelor's degree. This means community college and university libraries are now serving high-school students. In turn, high-school librarians are now supporting and serving students who are in dual credit and college classes, and creating programs that will meet their needs, as well.

In order to craft programming that will help teens be successful, it is important for librarians who serve teens to gain perspectives from academic librarians. Librarians in schools and public libraries can collaborate with a K–16 point of view to bring forth programs that expose teens to college resources and grow the knowledge and skills of teens. Many university libraries have first-year experience librarians. These librarians provide instruction, programs, and services catered to freshman students; and students who may have spent time in the workforce and/or the military, and are returning to school to pursue their education and better their circumstances.

To this end, Valerie interviewed two academic librarians: Dr. Cynthia Charles at Dillard University and LaMoya Burks at Texarkana College.

LIBRARIAN SPOTLIGHT

Dr. Cynthia Charles, Director of the Will W. Alexander Library at Dillard University in New Orleans, Louisiana

Valerie Tagoe: Describe your library and the population it serves.

Cynthia Charles: Dillard University has a small enrollment, approximately 1,300. Before Hurricane Katrina, the enrollment was approximately 2,500. The university is affiliated with the United Methodist Church. Many students are from the New Orleans area and states such as Alabama, California, Florida, [and] Illinois (Chicago area).

VT: Do you have students from area high schools taking college courses on campus?

CC: Dillard has a relationship with two-year colleges like Delgado and high schools in Louisiana. Information services are available, [and] so is instruction.

VT: Do you have first-year experience librarians?

CC: Yes, only three librarians. Instruction is provided by request of professors. The ACE Center helps freshmen and sophomores, and sets up sessions for students. Introverts visit the Ace Center frequently.

VT: How do you market or publicize programming to freshmen and other populations?

CC: The library is open to the community through programming like book clubs, author visits, one-book, [and] One New Orleans. In the future, we are looking at redesigning the commons on the second floor of the library.

VT: What are your go-to resources when planning and executing programs for your library?

CC: Our literacy programs.

VT: How do you market or publicize programming to this population?

CC: It is done through our Black History Month programming.

VT: What are the results that you have seen so far from programs you enacted for your first-year experience students?

CC: Outreach. Programming draws students in, especially an event we do with the Baby Dolls, a group of African American men and women carnival masters. Hosting events helps students see ways to reach out to the community. Dr. Eartha Johnson started the Tuesday Tea, a faculty-author series. If faculty travels outside the country, they come and lecture about their travels at the library. Other programs are Take Back the Night domestic violence awareness program, and the open mic in partnership with Tulane University, Loyola University, and Xavier University.

VT: How do you integrate technology into all library programming aspects: promotion of programs, delivery of programs, and assessment of library programming?

CC: Social media, but Facebook and Twitter have a larger reach. We concentrate on promoting programming.

VT: What can K–12 librarians do to better prepare students?

CC: At the university level, we are able to target instruction outside of instruction time, because students can attend events in the evenings, after classes. This is something that K–12 librarians may consider doing. They can also develop something for parents to show what we (libraries and librarians) can provide. K–12 librarians can also prepare students by teaching them security online, how to be safe online.

LIBRARIAN SPOTLIGHT
LaMoya Burks, Head Librarian at Texarkana College in Texarkana, Texas

Valerie Tagoe: Describe your library and the population it serves.

LaMoya Burks: Our library serves all students, seeing [as] we are community-college higher education. We range from development education, which has a bridge with GED to allow students the opportunity to transition to our campus for admissions. We also have honors cohorts, general admissions, early admissions, continuing education [and] even workforce education. Many of our students are first-generation, at-risk, underserved populations. Our library supports all programs, both print and electronically; programming ranges include all programs; and our library is open to all students. We often refer to the building as the Academic Commons building, seeing [as] tutoring, reference services, disability support, testing, advisement, and retention are all housed in the building.

VT: How do you market or publicize programming to these populations?

LB: As senior librarian, for the past six years I have led the library instruction and much of the outreach services. Through both, I design and implement lectures, workshops, and creative engagement activities to support student development. I work closely with instructors to stay abreast of curriculum to ensure the library continues to be resourceful.

VT: What results are you are seeing so far from programs you enacted for your first-year experience students?

LB: I am able to connect with students one on one, [in a] group, [in] class groups, and even as a way to follow up when using electronic resources. Students seek validation that they are completing what is necessary and are building skills necessary for their next step in coursework. As stated above, the library helps to secure confidence in the academic journey.

VT: What do students expect from libraries and librarians?

LB: Students expect the library to be available as a space, to connect to studies, [and] to have available tools to allow them to continue to study according to the diverse way[s] students learn.

VT: What can K–12 librarians do to better prepare students?

LB: K–12 librarians can seek to assist students in introducing them to skills necessary on their higher education journey. The databases and research strategies are areas that can be introduced. Together, both sectors can bridge a stronger student dynamic to success. Basic research strategy can be introduced at the grade-school level, and once entering academia, the next step in the depth of assessment and, for example, writing skill can be achieved. The collaboration of both sectors to make skills and tool usage normalized across all grade levels would be an asset. Further, we should seek to include library resources not as an additional area to entertain students but as more of a subject area for students as [young] as kindergarten. It is very necessary to not separate literacy from traditional subject areas. Students must know very early on the endless possibilities all libraries present. The school library must become the centralized component in housing talent, development, leisure, and enrichment consistently.

Collaboration with College and University Librarians

There is a great deal of talk and action surrounding the school library and public library connection and collaboration. However, school and public librarians may not consider collaborating with college and university librarians. Yet they all serve the same communities in varying ways, so why not join forces? The interviews with LaMoya Burks and Dr. Cynthia Charles can help librarians who serve teens think of instruction, technology, marketing, and programming in different ways. College and university librarians can be a wealth of information, ideas, and resources when it comes to instruction, technology, and programming. Connecting with and collaborating with academic librarians can be a powerful programming booster. Imagine the programming possibilities from writing workshops, cultural and art programs, research workshops ... The potential to take programming to another dimension is there and can help bridge the distance that teens and their parents may have from middle school and high school to college—not to mention the research possibilities and taking a scientific examination of the effect of programming and the impact of library programs on student learning as students move from secondary school to college, the university, and the workforce.

Key Points

In an *Education Week* interview with Django Paris and Sammy Alim about their book *Culturally Sustaining Pedagogies: Teaching and Learning for Justice in a Changing World*, the authors stated:

> Culturally sustaining pedagogy exists wherever education sustains lifeways of communities who have been and continue to be damaged and erased through schooling. (Ferlazzo, 2019)

As libraries are places where librarians hold the power to inform, curate, disseminate, and organize information in ways that will continue to oppress or uplift and liberate, it is essential to be intentional about creating spaces where everyone is welcome.

- Educational spaces have historically been tools of colonization.

- Librarians must be intentional about creating spaces where all funds of knowledge are recognized and uplifted.

- Learners will prioritize engaging with narratives that affirm their views of the world. Expanding that knowledge by looking for intersections between adjacent and distant groups is a way to spark curiosity.

- Remember that the work of inclusion isn't only about race or external identity markers, as plenty of individuals experience oppression and marginalization or erasure based on aspects of their identities that are invisible.

- Much of the work of welcoming everyone can be done through adjustments to three main areas of librarianship: classification systems, programming, and physical/virtual environment.

Reflection

- As a librarian, what do you do to welcome students and teens into the library space?

- Has creating a welcoming environment in which teens can be involved been a relevant factor in your planning, instruction, and programming?

- As you think about the future career and educational paths of the young people you serve, what programs are you creating to help them pursue their aspirations?

- Have you sought to collaborate with librarians at local community colleges and universities?

CHAPTER 3

Making It Work

Now that you have an idea of what new programs will be brought to the library or the existing programs that will be livened up, the next question is how to make it work. Some ideas to consider for making your programming successful:

- Consider the standards and how inclusion of the standards will help make the case for funding library programming to decision-makers and other stakeholders.

- Think about the availability of resources to execute programs. What do you have access to? What resources do you need or would like to have to broaden the impact of library programs?

- What funding is needed to procure the supplies, technology, and advertising for the programs?

- How will you market and advocate for the programs?

The following sections will explore each of these areas in further detail.

Standards or No Standards: That Is the Question

Program development can be either standards tied to curriculum or based on a theme, season, holiday, or trend. In the age of data-driven instruction and proving your worth/showing your value, school librarians in particular must look at library programming and instruction with the standards-based lens and connect that work to how it impacts campus improvement and student achievement test scores.

School library programming encapsulates all of this: curriculum, trends/current events, and standards, be it state curriculum standards, college and career-readiness standards, AASL, Future Ready, and ISTE Standards. Programming can also be extracurricular-based, especially if a librarian sponsors a club. At every opportunity, school librarians should develop programming with standards in mind. This can be a powerful advocacy tool because school librarians can demonstrate how they extend student learning with every activity or action that takes place within the walls of the school library day in and day out.

Public libraries can take a different approach to library programs, as they are not beholden to curricular and instructional goals. For example, public libraries, although they are not held to curriculum and state standards, they do have to provide reports to the community at city council meetings, develop strategic plans and long-range plans for servicing the community, and may provide reports to a state association. For example, public libraries in Texas provide annual reports to the Texas Municipal Library Directors Association. However, public librarians may find it beneficial to implement standards-based programming in their libraries for children and teens, and collaborate with school librarians in doing so.

Public librarians may find that applying or making standards part of their programming helps demonstrate that they, too, are helping teen patrons achieve learning goals outside the school and aids in the mission to cultivate lifelong learning. This would result in a win for the public library and a win for the schools in that the public library in its partnership with the schools and school libraries helps meet not just the information needs of the community, but the learning and academic needs of the community as well.

Public libraries can also communicate to their boards and other stakeholders how they assist schools, and to parents how they, too, advance or deepen the learning of young people in the community. Public libraries also have another advantage in that they have budgets specifically for programming, whereas school libraries do not.

School librarians are often tasked with searching for low-cost or no-cost library programming, writing grants, holding fund-raisers, or even using their own pocketbooks to cover the costs of library programs, which in itself can be a challenge.

Show Me the Money

In terms of funding, if librarians had their way, the sky would be the limit. If the sky were the limit, what would your vision be in terms of program delivery, advertising and promotion, gauging and assessing impact, etc.? Teens are great sources to consult with in terms of providing input on library programming with a "sky's the limit" mindset. They are extremely imaginative and creative. In Valerie's experience, teens have provided ideas for programming, come up with ways to secure supplies, and assisted in program promotion. That being said, if funding or lack thereof presents an obstacle, here are some things to consider:

- What essential elements of the program can easily be provided and performed in order to make it work?

- How can funding be secured to help liven up the program and sustain it into the future?

In order to enrich and sustain library programs, school and public librarians often have to raise funds or write grants to secure funding on their own. Over the course of two years, Valerie collaborated with a team of gardeners at a public library program. Valerie worked with a team of volunteer gardeners to create an educational program surrounding gardening, and grant writing played a major role in funding aspects of the program: seeds, soil, books, notebooks, and signage all had to be purchased in order to bring the program to the public. She worked with the gardeners to draft a grant proposal and ask grant-makers to "Show me the money."

Valerie's advice for writing grant proposals is to be specific. List what is needed (supplies, technology, etc.) and make sure to include the who, what, when, and where:

- Who: the demographic information of the tweens and teens who will be served

- What: the programming funded by the grant

- When: a timeline of the program activities

- Where: where the teens live and the service area of your library

Also list what your organization can provide and what the grant-maker can fund.

Funding sources for library grants can come from a myriad of places, and it is a challenge to decide exactly where to start. There are many organizations that provide funding for both central and classroom school libraries. Following are some ideas of where to look.

Crowdfunding

Many school librarians look to crowdfunding sites like Donors Choose for library projects with a supply need of $500 to $1,000. Donors Choose often has initiatives at different times of the year in which benefactors may fund programs in a particular area or school district at one time. In order to maximize the possibilities of crowdfunding, draft grants for projects that cost from $500 to $1,000 to execute and then post the projects at the most opportune times. The crowdfunding sites often send out emails or post to their websites or social media pages when there are special initiatives, such as matching donations or having a specific dollar amount covered for a project.

LIBRARIAN SPOTLIGHT

Lovie Howell, Librarian at Benton Middle School in Benton, Louisiana

Donors Choose in conjunction with Sonic Drive-In has been a great way to raise funds when the budget is waning. Social media accounts—including Facebook, Instagram, Twitter, and the school app—help spread the word about what you are raising funds for. Parents, students, and community members are able to get involved with very little effort using these channels. This connection also helps our local Sonic Drive-In prosper and gives us the opportunity to give back locally. Donors Choose makes it very easy to write a grant and gives multiple examples of great grants that have been funded. They also walk you through the Thank You process, where you can set up a station to have the student patrons involved in writing the thank yous. I have written and been generously granted almost $11,000 since 2010.

Look Local

Beyond Donors Choose, Valerie has found that looking locally is a viable option for funding school and public library programming. Start with cities and municipalities. It's important to learn about all initiatives and partnerships that exist in cities and municipalities, as they may award grants to schools and other entities. Local agencies and nonprofits can also be a source of funding. School and public libraries may have to work in tandem with a friend's group or a school district foundation that functions as a 501C3.

501C3 organizations can enter into contracts and accept funds on behalf of the library, whereas public libraries and school district libraries may not be able to enter into contracts in order to accept grant funds. Local organizations and nonprofit organizations may also provide grants to school and public libraries. For example, some local chapters of the Junior League fund programming in libraries.

Lastly, networking locally will also help make community connections that will help fund or bolster library programs. As librarians write grant proposals to local grant-makers, they may be able to network with various organizations and businesses that will lead to other open doors and opportunities to liven up your library through programming. Local organizations may be able to refer you to other organizations, agencies, and businesses that can possibly fund programs and provide resources for library programming.

Look National

Businesses with operations across the country can also serve as a source of funding for programming. Many large corporations provide grant programs through their charitable-giving foundations and donate items to organizations like schools and public libraries. Volunteers and community liaisons can help make the connection to local businesses. A visit to the websites of businesses can provide valuable information on grant opportunities. Many businesses operate on a giving cycle, so be sure to check to see when they accept letters of interest and applications for various grant programs.

Grant Reporting

As you are writing grants, be sure to have a plan to gather information on programs to provide a report to the grant-makers. Even if it is not a requirement of a grant, it is best practice to write a report and provide insight on how many people the program served, how the funds were used, as well as reaction and feedback from program participants.

 LIBRARIAN SPOTLIGHT

Daniela Lankford, Librarian at Klein Oak High School in Spring, Texas

In Texas, homecoming is a big deal, and so are the chrysanthemums, or mums, traditionally given at games and other events. But think about the money, and the landfill space if you only use them once. At my high school we collect used, or "vintage" mums and re-sell them every year. We remove the names from the ribbons, leaving the rest up to the buyer to fix or customize. It's great because we make money for the homecoming charity. We raise about $1,000 every year, and the donations come in year-round. I store them in large plastic tubs labeled with $25, $50, $75, and $100 on the outside. This makes for easy access and we don't have to sort every year. Our student council members "model" the mums at lunch in the time leading up to homecoming, and they make a slide presentation to advertise to parents on the school website.

STEAM and Makerspaces

Integrating STEM, STEAM, and makerspaces has become a major part of library programming in the last decade. The addition of instruction on the use of STEAM and makerspaces requires both literacy and application of the sciences. The flexible spaces that are available in libraries make them optimal for STEAM, STEM, and makerspace activities and programming. Popular makerspace activities include:

- LEGO walls

- button making

- arts and crafts activities like knitting clubs, make and take Valentines, a teen spin on painting with a twist (if facilities permit)

- costume creations for cosplay events

- coding with Sphero

- projects on Code.org

- 3D printing workshops

- podcasting stations

These kinds of programs also provide an opportunity for librarians to be involved in technology education at all levels and ages—elementary, middle, and high school—and possibly provide exposure to tech education that students may not receive in the classroom due to course of study, graduation plan, and even availability of courses or lack thereof in some communities. Libraries are uniquely poised to provide teens exposure through STEAM and makerspace programming that they may not receive otherwise.

Sources of Funding for STEAM and Makerspace Programs

Librarians have turned to organizations and companies such as Code.org and LEGO to obtain training and resources for STEAM and makerspace programs. Following are some places to look.

Code.org has provided professional development to librarians in the past through the Regional Education Service Centers located throughout the state of Texas. Visit the website to see available options: bit.ly/3CTmevz. Librarians can also sign up to learn how they can teach computer science skills to students.

LEGO Education partners with school districts to provide supplies and professional development to librarians who wish to use LEGO in their maker-spaces. See funding opportunities on their website: bit.ly/3ImH2Na

As part of its strategic goals, the Institute of Museum and Library Services seeks to champion lifelong learning and strengthen community engagement. Search for grant opportunities and how to apply on their website: imls.gov/grants/grant-programs.

Professional organizations are also a valuable resource for professional development and training on STEAM and makerspace programs. Librarians across the country attend ISTE conferences and professional development offerings to keep pace with trends in technology instruction and makerspace innovations.

In addition to ISTE, state professional organizations are also excellent sources for STEAM and makerspace program ideas. In Texas, many librarians attend the Texas Computer Education Association annual conference, along with their workshops and district meetings, to gain certifications and learn about the latest in tech they can bring back to their campuses in the form of programming, as well as in instruction, library management, and more.

Marketing and Library Program Advocacy

One of the most crucial parts of library program advocacy is gathering data from patrons to inform library programming and presenting that data in a way that communicates the correct messages to those in their community. In Julia's experience, amplifying student voices has been one of the most effective ways to get buy-in from those in her community.

She began with a survey about "Reading Tastes and Habits," which revealed that though over 70% of the more than 800 students surveyed felt that reading would be important for their lives after the close of their K–12 education, fewer than 70% of them self-identified as readers. The survey revealed other interesting statistics, too, like the fact that many students did not read books they were assigned in class.

Contrary to popular belief, it is possible to progress throughout the school system without reading assigned books. However, it doesn't seem possible to navigate the complex layers of literacy necessary in order to participate completely in society without having an intimate and continuously nurtured relationship with words and language. The fourteenth Librarian of Congress, Carla Hayden, has said, "Libraries are a cornerstone of democracy—where information is free and equally available to everyone. People tend to take that for granted, and then they don't realize what is at stake when that is put at risk" (Orenstein, 2003). This is to say that we are ultimately jeopardizing someone's ability to access free information and participate in a democratic society when we don't protect their right to not only have a library, but regularly engage with all that a library has to offer.

One of the ways the community went about gathering support for the reopening of the Montbello branch of the Denver Public Library was through the media and social media (Asmar, 2018). There were a few community activists on social media and one particularly involved educator (Randall Duval) who posted videos and other content about the lack of having a library. This led to serious discussion among the school leaders within the building about what it might take to reopen the library. From there, the district library director, Caroline Hughes, and the regional library director, Janet Damon, led efforts to remodel and revamp the library. It was through their leadership that the library got a $150,000 redesign and a new collection of updated and culturally relevant texts. After the library reopening, we continued to build community by establishing Facebook groups, an Instagram page, and a hashtag #MontbelloReads to curate information about what we were reading and the events we undertook. The documentation of library programs on social media is an important part of library advocacy. However, student data privacy concerns are important to consider, as are the ethical implications of building a social media presence as individuals for the work we do with young people.

When creating a plan for advocacy, one might ask the following questions:

1. Who are your primary stakeholders?

2. How can you amplify the voices of young people in order to more effectively advocate for their needs?

3. What resources will you need on an ongoing basis (for example, book club books for a #TrueBookFair)?

4. How might you enlist the help of those in leadership?

Donations

Collecting advance reader copies (ARCs) and donations is one way to contribute to #TrueBookFairs. Created by Mount Vernon librarian Julie Stivers these events allow students to get free books and diminish the divide between those who have the resources to purchase from traditional book fairs and those who do not. Here are a few sources of donations:

 Book Love Foundation (booklovefoundation.org) is a nonprofit that provides classroom libraries to language arts teachers through a yearly grant cycle application, review, and approval process. The foundation also provides professional development as well as a summer book club.

 The Molina Foundation's Book Buddies program (molinafoundation.org/programs/book-buddies) provides thousands of new books to schools and community organizations working with under-served communities.

 First Book (firstbook.org) works with publishers to drastically reduce the cost of newly published books so that Title 1 schools can afford to purchase them in large quantities.

 Black Men Read (blackmenreadnow.com) is an organization led by Black men with a focus on empowerment through literacy. They aim to "ignite social change by creating opportunities through literacy within Black communities."

 Bring Me A Book (bringmeabook.org) works with partner schools to give young people free copies of books they choose. They believe that "book access, reading agency, identity, and choice are equity in action and keys to avid reading."

Fundraising/User Feedback Surveys

It's a good idea to make sure you don't have too many questions on surveys, because it can begin to feel like an assessment if there are more than a student can answer comfortably and quickly. Vary the question format as well; use Likert scales, drop-down boxes, and other options that will allow Google forms to aggregate user data that can then be used for advocacy.

Questions for User Feedback Surveys

- I am interested in these types of reading (check all that apply).
- I feel comfortable/uncomfortable about my ability to check out books from the library.
- How many books did you read independently last year?
- Of these, how many did you finish?
- How do you feel about reading?
- Reading is boring (agree/disagree).
- Reading is important (agree/disagree).
- Do you think reading for pleasure will be important for your life after MS/HS?
- Do you think reading academically will be important for your life after MS/HS?
- Do you consider yourself to be a reader?
- Why or why not?
- How often do you read outside of school?
- What is the best book you've ever read?
- Why do you like it so much?

Budgeting

Though much of the budgeting that happens is at the administrative levels and above, there are ways to get additional funds for the library through advocacy work and fundraising.

In Julia's experience, she has applied to her district giving foundation for their yearly grant cycle and used the proceeds for book club titles. She has also been granted funds in the past for excellence in materials circulation, as well as participating in our culturally responsive libraries cohort. For the latter, a district pilot of librarians came together as a sort of think-tank, performing collection audits and putting their heads together to come up with new titles. Then, when the extra funds were allocated, every library in the district had somewhere to begin when considering top titles that should be a part of every collection. Collection development specialists worked to make sure each library collection reflects the demographics of the student population.

After receiving funds, it's good to solicit input from administrators, staff, and students. Some questions you might start with are:

- What do they want to see in the collection?
- What plans do they have for curriculum that utilizes library resources?
- How can I best work together with them to support yearly goals and independent reading?

Julia typically purchases materials first that are in high circulation and frequently unreturned. Next, she prioritizes replacement or duplicate copies for materials that have been damaged or have been requested by specific individuals. Recently, she has begun to make more purchases of ebooks and audio book licenses in greater numbers because in her school community, every student has a Chromebook, so access to a digital collection in Sora is in high demand, especially among middle school students.

Displays and labeling are another important part of budgeting. What types of displays will you have? What labeling will you use for your library? Is it genrefied, and if so, do you need signage in different languages? Consider allocating a portion of the budget to creating interactive displays and those that showcase student artwork, as well as those that gather feedback from the community about reading choices, tastes, and habits. When thinking about displays, consider the 3D, versus the 5D, display. A 3D display has library materials as objects and perhaps some wording or questions that will get a user thinking. A 5D display takes the experience further with interactive pieces like QR codes with sound clips of library patrons giving their reviews; quotes or interactive video clips from film adaptations of books; a sound bar where users can listen to audio book clips; or QR codes that link to online resources to take the learning further.

Another part of budgeting is programming that reflects the needs of teachers and students. Every year, Julia conducts a survey to gather feedback about library visits and whether they met teachers' needs. She's been fortunate to have author visits, field trips, and book club funds supplemented by administrative funds, as well as generous donations from community members. Never underestimate the desire community members have to connect young people with good books when the members are given a specific project to support. Many people like to create Little Free Libraries in their communities, and there have been some creative constructions both in private neighborhoods and on school property. In the same vein that young people love to come together to create a community garden, a Little Free Library feeds the community's intellect.

WE DO THIS IN COMMUNITY
What Actions Can Adults Take?

In a school community, it is vital that we see school librarians as more than individuals who circulate books. The experience of having a highly effective school library is immersive and can result in a lifelong relationship with words and language that transforms individuals, the communities they live in, and society. Unfortunately, there has been a global decline in support for libraries as a whole and school libraries specifically, despite the fact that research shows, "When schools have high-quality library programs and librarians who share their expertise with the entire school community, student achievement gets a boost" (Lance & Kachel, 2018). The recent SLIDE report is conducts research into "the continuing, national decline in school librarian positions and how school districts decide to staff library, learning resources, and instructional technology programs for K–12 students" (2018). Though the research is ongoing, it has already determined that in 2018–2019, at least one-fifth of US school districts had no librarians. A large part of what adults can do is support advocacy. Inform yourself about library staffing and support beyond the K–6 level and beyond your immediate community. Resource hoarding is real and so is misallocation of funds. Many students in secondary schools are aliterate, meaning they technically can read, but choose not to because of the elimination of choice, time, and access to high-quality, culturally relevant reading materials.

 SLIDE Report
(libslide.org)

 ASCD: Engaging Middle School Readers with Access and Choice (bit.ly/37C4Kbz)

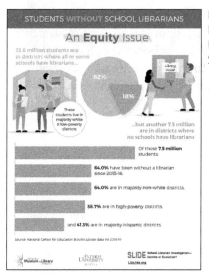

Figure 3.1 Students Without Librarians: An Equity Issue. Source: National Center for Education Statistics/State data for 2018-19.

 Julie Torres and Julie Stivers on "Healing Reading Trauma" at ALA20 (bit.ly/37MVVvT)

Other than advocating for full-time, certified teacher librarians or training-and-certification programs for library technicians, adults can support young people by participating in book donation drives for #TrueBookFairs—book fairs that do not require money to be exchanged. They are made possible by donations, including the generous donations of ARCS from publishers, or books the school purchases at a discount and then gives to students for free. North Carolina librarian, Julie Stivers (@BespokeLib), is a master at organizing and carrying out #TrueBookFairs. Learn more by reading the blog post recapping her ALA20 session with Julia.

It is also important for parents to participate in book clubs and read books the young people in their lives are reading. All too often, parents determine that books they have not read do not belong in schools. Before participating in the development of policies that limit intellectual freedom and ban books, students themselves should be asked about the books they have read that have changed their lives. In this way, a library collection and programming to support it truly involves the voices of all stakeholders.

Practical Ways to Engage Readers

- Coordinate book drives to occur alongside Back to School Night or student-led conferences.
- Post QR codes with student and staff book reviews around the school.
- Invite local authors to do virtual or in-person school visits. Have students vote about whom they would like to invite.
- Conduct "One-Book-One-School" initiatives and invite students to host community conversations in multiple languages.
- Invite young people to speak at board meetings about their experiences reading books that have been banned or those that are being considered by community leaders as "inappropriate" for school settings.
- Cover classroom doors or other school surfaces with the covers of books that are well known and loved by community members.

Get Creative

As a school librarian, Julia often wished for times when people would take a creative approach to a literacy curriculum rooted in student empowerment. She was always hopeful we would eventually learn to let go of some of the things we do simply because they are always what has been done. As Julia sees it, school is a place where we should emulate the way people develop and maintain literate lives after they leave the K–12 school system. But we should also be free to think creatively in imagining more for future generations than we have experienced ourselves. So what does an adult's literary life look like?

In her article "Skim Reading Is the New Normal, and the Effect on Society Is Profound" (2018), Maryanne Wolf mentions the way that so many modern readers tend to "taste" books and snippets of information online they find interesting, only diving deeper if or when there is content throughout a work to keep them engaged. It isn't unusual for readers to read part of many books, versus an entire book start to finish. Additionally, though audiobooks and ebooks are very popular, physical books still remain the reading of choice for many young people.

We know that many adult readers ebb and flow with their reading fluency. And so communicating to young people that it is normal to have times in our lives when we are "better" at reading, and times when we may not feel able to finish traditional books, is an important part of reframing conversations about readers and reading identity. All too often, many young readers feel inadequate because of the tests they take and the scores they get, or the shaming that happens because of the free-reading choices they make. We can change this when we seek their input about what they like to read, give them what they want, and protect their time to read it.

Keeping in mind the fact that physical books are still the top format young readers choose means we must think of creative ways to engage young people in the act of participating in and maintaining a school-wide culture of reading. It is essential that reading role models and those with established reading habits be recruited and supported as mentors for younger readers. One way to diminish psychological barriers that exist among cohorts of young people pertains to the many stigmas and negativity biases that can develop when reading has been habitually commodified within the school system. We have to help readers find the books that interest them and encourage them to read fluently and continuously, no matter the Lexile level of the book. As we know, Lexile is not the only indicator of text complexity, and there are many indicators that are not quantifiable that can be documented and used to support readers as they seek challenge.

Adult readers independently seek challenge when they have a purpose for reading that aligns with their interests. It is possible to engage young learners by appealing to their interests and including authentic assessments as a culminating activity after they finish reading a book. Some examples of authentic and non-authentic assessments are shared in table 3.1.

Table 3.1 Examples of Authentic and Non-Authentic Assessments

AUTHENTIC	INAUTHENTIC
Book club facilitation with guiding questions, takeaways, and visual or other media presentation.	Book report or book summary for teacher assessment.
Community watch-club in the library featuring a book/movie pairing and post-screening discussion led by students.	Watching a documentary; whole-class reading of a book with an analysis essay or short-answer written responses.
Community night with invited stakeholders participating in voter information and registration, as well as student-prepared multimedia presentations about voter registration and disenfranchisement.	Research project that culminates in a research paper and slides presentation for the class to view.
Student-compiled vertical book-stacks that are thematically connected with book talks and rationales for why readers should choose these books (Torres, 2021).	Teacher- or librarian-prepared cart with books and teacher conducted read-alouds.

Tools for Matching Books with Readers

Use these online tools to help match readers with their perfect book.

 Epic Reads Quiz: "Pick a Bunch of Books & We'll Reveal Your Book Aesthetic" (epicreads.com/blog/book-aesthetic-quiz)

 Book Riot: "What YA Book Should I Read Next?" (bookriot. com/ya-book-quiz)

 Buzzfeed: "We'll Give You a YA Book to Read Based on Your Book Preferences" (bzfd.it/3pavkhZ)

 Gnooks: Discover New Books (gnooks.com) Input authors you know and like and let the AI recommend others you might like.

You can also discover your next read by using Goodreads or your favorite online bookstore. Begin by searching for books you like and see what comes up as a similar or recommended title.

───────────○───────────

There are numerous ways to keep programming creative and engaging for both students and community members outside the physical school building, but they have to be rooted in what Paulo Freire has termed "education as a practice of liberation." In other words, each time students engage with books and library programming, they are engaging with the part of themselves that wants to be free—free to think, free to shape the world into the one they want, free to question what they don't like about their society, and free to redefine their place in it.

Sustaining a Library Program for Everyone

In order to sustain a library program for everyone, it truly does take everyone doing their part. School leadership has to support allocation of appropriate funds that support a robust and vibrant library program with interactive experiences, as well as engaging materials—beyond makerspaces. Librarians and library professionals must regularly communicate with administrators and staff in order to be able to fit library programming in with the overall mission and vision for student achievement within the organization. Staff must work with librarians to make time for independent reading and think creatively about the ways young people engage with the act of reading that are very different from how reading may have looked in generations past. Students can work together with community members and stakeholders to imagine and create events for people of all ages, regardless of ability, age, language proficiency, or experience with library spaces. In a community with a library that is centered around a practice of empowerment and liberation, young people are at the heart of events, their ideas are reflected in every display, and their likenesses adorn the cover of most books.

Key Points

The practical elements of school library programming are changing with the times. Marketing and advocacy now often include a social media manager component. Due to funding shortages, many library programs are defunded or underfunded, which necessitates creative approaches to fundraising and boosting awareness about the connections between effective library programming and curricular student achievement. In many spaces, students themselves are able to take key leadership positions as reading role models, library aides, and junior librarians, and even facilitators of community forums. Considering the ways all stakeholders can become invested in the longevity of a school library program is a step toward community interdependence.

- Gather feedback from students and use for advocacy, information, and transforming curricular practices to incorporate independent reading lessons and units of study.

- Involve students in the planning and execution of social media promotion in authentic, rather than performative, ways.

- Remember to supplement your budget with grants and community partnerships. Consider displays and other interactive elements of your library space as budget line items as well.

- Adults can help by becoming informed about methods for collaboration with the library, as well as participating in community read-ins and discussions about books that are being considered for curriculum adoption or are up for reconsideration due to censorship.

- Student facilitation of community discussions, together with creative reimagining of the role of a school library and librarian, will sustain a library that operates through and for liberation.

Reflection

- How will you include students in library programming and help cultivate their skills as leaders?

- What resources can you tap to sustain programming you design and implement?

- What community members can be considered a resource for your programming? How can they be authentically included in processes like collection development so their reading tastes and habits are considered too?

CHAPTER 4

The Program Is Done ... Now What?

First, is a program ever truly done? One of the most important aspects of being in a school environment is that things are always changing. It's important for us to remember that part of living in schools as professionals is that we are open and willing to change with the times, because our students will also change with the times. According to the National Education Statistics website, by the year 2022 (the year of this book's publication), the majority of students in American public schools will identify as multiracial, multiethnic, or non-white. Even so, the majority of America's public school teachers identify as white (see figure 4.1).

These statistics identify not only a racial and cultural disconnect, but also a need for deep understanding of, respect for, and curiosity about ways of working with and educating students from across the spectrum of what might be considered "culturally diverse populations." Furthermore, as community demographics change, and the role of school changes, librarians and library professionals have a professional responsibility to adapt what we do to meet the needs of our users in ways that are timely, culturally responsive, and responsive to the needs of adult professionals in our rapidly changing world.

Figure 4.1 Racial and ethnic makeup of US public school teachers and students has changed over time. Source: Pew Research Center (2021).

Statuses and Trends in the Education of Racial and Ethnic and Linguistic Groups (nces.ed.gov/programs/raceindicators)

The Importance of Libraries as Intellectual Spaces

Libraries and librarians are for more than checking out books. Some additional functions and tasks that librarians and library professionals undertake are shared in table 4.1 below.

Table 4.1 Additional Functions and Tasks

FUNCTION	TASKS
Circulation	Check in/Check out materials
	Process holds and renewals
	Provide ways for students to encounter information "in the wild" or independently via displays and self check-out
	Run circulation reports and share results with the community with the goal of fostering independence, rather than dependence
Collection Management	Sort and shelve materials
	Shift collections
	Shelf-read (walk the shelves to see what is out of place and make newer or high-demand titles visible by displaying covers out)
	Process materials by adding genre label stickers and creating spine labels
	Weed the collection
	Protect intellectual freedom
	Reflect on the cultural relevancy of the Dewey Decimal system or genre and classification systems
Resource Sharing	Process ILL requests
	Monitor and process requests from users
	Return misplaced books to their rightful homes
Other Duties	Regularly communicate with district library services
	Attend and facilitate professional development with a PLN (professional learning network)
	Maintain signage and monitor its effectiveness
	Manage physical environment (including COVID safety protocols)

Continued

FUNCTION	TASKS
Maintain Virtual Library Environment	Create digital collections specific to the user population
	Display circulation statistics and most popular titles for users to browse
	Ensure the database accurately reflects available physical materials
	Update with library programming information and most frequently requested services

Adapted from Hirsch, S. (2018). *Information Services Today: An Introduction, Second Edition.*

When thinking about the different tasks librarians and library professionals have responsibility for, it is still astounding to me that so many places have opted not to have librarians or library professionals in library spaces.

One of the most beneficial aspects of library spaces and programs that are well-staffed and run is that the users (students) are able to fully utilize the space as a resource and benefit in the way Ta-Nehisi Coates describes in his 2015 work *Between the World and Me*:

> The pursuit of knowing was freedom to me, the right to declare your own curiosities and follow them through all manner of books. I was made for the library, not the classroom. The classroom was a jail of other people's interests. The library was open, unending, free. Slowly, I was discovering myself. (p. 48)

Advocacy

Advocacy for library programming and staffing in *all* educational environments is crucial because *all* young people have the right to explore and have their knowledge of and relationship with words nurtured. The demographics of who is staffing libraries and feeling most comfortable in them most likely will not change dramatically until the mindset of those with the power to fund (or defund) them does.

When libraries are valued in learning communities, and the people who staff them are well-supported, we are able to create spaces where libraries aren't just a place for books to get checked out and checked back in, but rather spaces where students are able to unlock the full potential of their creative minds and function as individuals able to contribute to and analyze the increasingly complex world they live in. If we say all kids can and should have access to intellectual thought, then we defend the right for *all* young people, not just the privileged few, to exist and thrive within such spaces.

Social Media Advocacy

Most libraries by now understand the importance of including some sort of online advocacy for the library space so the community becomes informed about what's available in the library and what's actually going on. In Julia's experience with the Montbello branch of the Denver Public Library, she used the hashtag #MontbelloReads to capture what students were reading and doing, and general goings-on at the library. This eventually moved to a Facebook page to get the students a bit more involved with community advocacy. Along the way, Julia documented much of what went on in the library through her blog in the effort to bring more attention to the experience of those who are not necessarily traditionally trained as librarians, but are learning to do the job and serve students to the best of their ability with minimal resources.

Program Evaluation and Assessment

Often when programs are complete, assessment is often an afterthought. The focus tends to be on examining statistics, such as how many people attended, or reviewing the activities done to promote the program. Social media posts or engagement regarding a library program may also be taken into account. However, program assessment in all library types can and should go further in terms of determining the reach of the program by looking at demographics, such as:

- schools they attend (home, public, private);

- what patrons/students learned and how this learning impacts student academic performance; and

- how the program impacted literacy, college readiness, and standards and skills/workforce learning.

These and other valuable data can be ascertained through evaluation and assessment.

Program evaluation and assessment of STEM and makerspaces is vital for school and public library programs because teens will be learning skills that tie closely to what is taught in both K–12 and college classes. It's important to assess the impact of these programs by creating formative and summative assessment data to report to stakeholders and grant-makers (Wardrip et al., 2019). In creating data for programs, go beyond the statistics of how many students attended, date, time, etc. Include what state standards and national standards apply to the programs done in the library. This data should be readily available both on your institution platforms and personal platforms for safe-keeping. In creating assessments, think of the audience this data will be reported to and anticipate what questions they may have about what the students have learned and what the students would like to learn (Wardrip et al., 2019). Also have a post-program survey for the students to provide feedback on the program and to give comments about the skills learned and how they will use them now and in the future.

Collecting Data

When collecting data, all schools should have policies about protecting student privacy, which means information collected and displayed must be free of data such as student identification numbers, names, or any other easily identifiable information.

In a previous chapter, we discussed the importance of creating user feedback surveys that provide information to library populations and those who run them about how programming is working and whether the physical environment and services provided are actually doing the intended work of encouraging interdependence among users and independence for young people.

Julia likes to collect data by class so she can show teachers what their students have said about the roles of literacy in their lives (chapter 2) in addition to how they might best change their library programming in order to better serve the students as their needs change. One of Julia's favorite resources for explaining the shifting nature of student engagement with information comes from Troy Hicks and Kristen Hawley Turner in their book, *Connected Reading* (2015).

They provide a model (shown in figure 4.2) for consideration of the way students engage with information and materials that offers valuable insight for all educators and library and literacy professionals.

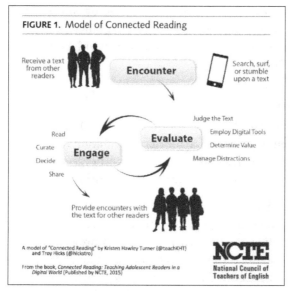

Figure 4.2 Model of Connected Reading. Source: Hicks, T. & Turner, K.H. (2015). *Connected Reading: Teaching Adolescent Readers in a Digital World.* Chamaign, IL: NCTE.

When we collect data, we should always go back to the question of how to make the data transparent for both adults *and* young people, and what they might be likely to do with the data after seeing it, as well as the emotional impact it might have on them. At best, data can be used as an advocacy tool to show those within learning communities about areas for growth. At worst, data is yet another way oppressive structures collect information that supports the continued use of oppressive structures to marginalize, disenfranchise, and erode the self-confidence of those operating within structures and systems that were not necessarily designed with their success in mind. How we encounter, engage with, and evaluate data is an important part of the continuing process of creating library programming that evolves with the times.

So, in essence, all data we collect might support these aims and serve as tools of advocacy and information around which we shift and grow our practice.

One consideration when collecting types of data is Radaganthan's Laws of Library Science, explained in table 4.2.

Table 4.2 Radaganthan's Laws of Library Science

ORIGINAL LAW	FURTHERMORE
Books are for use.	Ebooks, audiobooks, large-print books, and other materials are also for use and improve access.
Every reader his [or her/ their] book.	Every reader should have a similar experience in the library space, regardless of ability, identity markers, or previous library experience.
Every book its reader.	Every book or library material has a potential library user for which it will be the perfect fit. Encouraging readers to explore while also promoting various methods of sharing and recommending between them is essential.
Save the time of the user.	We can create systems that empower, rather than create dependence.
The library is a growing organism.	The library, its contents, and methods of providing services should change with the times, but at just the right pace so as not to seem outdated and so there are sustainable methods of educating users about their options and functionality. For example, for labels we use for the library, such as "library media center," "learning commons," or "campus library," what does the word "library" entail for your users in your specific time and place?

Adapted from Radaganthan, S.R. (1931). *Five Laws of Library Science.*

Reporting Format

Once you have program data, create a plan for how you will report it to various audiences: parents, stakeholders, administrators, board trustees, other departments within an institution, or partners outside the institution. This will range from a formal written report to a presentation utilizing popular software, complete with pictures, graphs, graphics, video, and sound clips or podcasts. If taking an educational research standpoint on reporting program data, consider Mills's guidelines for writing a research report, as well as format, style and conclusions/ thesis regarding the program (Mills, 2019). Utilize Microsoft and Google applications to create reports and create graphs and charts to display data. For instance, a chart or bar graph displaying the number of teens who participate in a coding program or book club discussion and their race/ethnicity can provide an instant at-a-glance snapshot of who participated in a technology education or literacy program—and its reach.

Seek Out Partnerships

Create and utilize partnerships within your institution and outside your institution for program assessment and evaluation. Following are some suggestions on where to start.

The Public Library

Team with the public library in your community to not only conduct joint programs but to assess and evaluate those programs. Public libraries may have access to assessment tools that school libraries do not. For example, many public libraries in Texas utilize the Counting Opinions platform to conduct surveys. Counting Opinions can also be used to obtain program evaluation data and feedback for joint programming. The use of these assessment tools can be mutually beneficial to both institutions, as both entities can partner together to conduct programs and then subsequently evaluate and assess program impact and outcomes.

Valerie has partnered with the local branch of the Dallas Public Library for getting the word out regarding public library card sign-up month. Students had the opportunity to sign up or renew their public library cards when Valerie invited them to set up a table in the cafeteria to conduct public library card sign-ups at lunch. This also allowed the public library staff to tell students and staff about upcoming and ongoing programs and services. Teens who were also eighteen years old had the opportunity to complete a voter registration card so they would be eligible to vote in the next election cycle. The public library staff shared the number of students who inquired about the library and the number of cards issued or renewed. Valerie in turn asked individual students to come to the school library individually to share if they renewed a card or were issued a new card. She then recognized the students for taking advantage of an important community resource: the public library.

Youth Serving Organizations

Seek out other organizations that serve youth and approach them about partnering on programs, as well as program assessment and evaluation. Youth-serving organizations and nonprofits may also have access to program assessment and evaluation tools and can also provide insight into community needs that the school, public, community college, or university library can fulfill. Librarians should be sure to obtain the proper permissions to work with these entities. If your institution already works with a nonprofit or youth-serving organization, insert the library into the narrative and leverage that existing partnership into the work you are doing as a librarian, then utilize any program and assessment tools they may already be using to gather data and assess the programs in the library, particularly if a program is in line with the existing partnership.

For example, if partnering with an organization regarding parent engagement, then create programs specifically for parents to utilize the library and its resources to fulfill their information needs: book and ebook circulation, database access, resume creation, job searches, college applications, training programs, and more.

Teen Council or Advisory Board

A teen council or advisory board can serve as a standing committee or focus group that will be used to provide feedback suggestions on program evaluation and assessment. The teen council/library advisory board can also assist in spreading the word about teen library programs and services to the greater community. The teens who participate should reflect the community served in order to provide a variety of perspectives, and they can give voice to the various information and educational needs of the community. They can also be a committee or board that reviews and provides insight on programming evaluation results and in turn provide their own honest conclusions and recommendations.

Creating Assessments for Programming

Create an assessment rubric or template that can be modified if needed for the type of program presented. Over time, formalize the assessment so the results can be reported not only to stakeholders but to decision-makers in the community, such as grant-makers or even university officials/departments you wish to partner with in terms of funding, programs, and instruction.

Take a Research Approach

In developing assessments, take a research approach to help focus the collection of data to answer questions that you as the librarian may have, as well as those the district or institution, stakeholders, funders/grant-makers, board members, legislators, and others who will bolster or fund and support library programming may have. Two books that come to mind in terms of research and assessment are *Educational Research Competencies for Analysis and Applications,* Twelfth Edition by Geoffery Mills and *Practical Research Planning and Design,* Twelfth Edition by Paul D. Leedy and Jeanne Ellis Ormond. Although these texts are used to teach research, they can aid librarians in creating assessments, analyzing and reporting data, developing conclusions about programs, and next steps.

Basic Program Assessment Template

The template shared in table 4.3 can be used to create an assessment for programming that is customized for your purposes.

Table 4.3 Program Assessment Template

INFORMATION	EXAMPLES
Demographic Information	Name (optional), age, race, education/school enrollment (public, private, home, etc.)
Date & Time	Date and time of program
Program Attended	Drop-down or short-answer
Likert Scale Questions	To determine level of knowledge and familiarity of concept before the program and after the program. For example, "Coding activity experience with coding: 1) None, 2) Some experience writing code, 3) Extensive experience (write code on a regular basis in class and at work), or 4) Expert (written code for class and/or work for one year or more)
Open-Ended Questions	Comments, statements, interviews, and other forms of feedback

Bringing It All Together

Community members and library users will continue to learn and grow together as the need for the services library professionals provide—and different actions we must take to best utilize library spaces—change. When we report program results to those in the community, it must always be with the utmost sensitivity toward making the programming better and advocating for buy-in from various stakeholder groups so they know, that even though the library is a public resource, it is often the private experiences users have within these spaces that shape their life-long relationships with words and their ability to fully and actively exercise their participatory citizenship.

The communal experiences we have with those within our PLNs lead to expanded abilities to grow as individual library professionals and model for young people what it means to learn and grow as part of a community that is simultaneously learning and growing. Social media posts are a part of documenting the activities and exciting moments we experience in library spaces for posterity and for the larger world. They also serve as a quick advocacy tool for friends of libraries who may want to contribute to programming in monetary or other ways. Furthermore, as mentioned in chapter 2, social media can be an extremely powerful way to combat efforts to squash intellectual freedom in library spaces.

Some questions to ask yourself after your library program feels ready to undertake:

- What library users are best served or centered by current practices and collections?

- Who is left out, and how can I best modify my daily practices to assist them?

- How can I modify the five laws of library science to fit my library community as it evolves and changes?

- Who do I learn from and what gaps are in my understanding as a result? How can I expand my circle of mentors and model mentorship practices for young people?
- What systems have I developed to have young people serve as mentors for one another?

Table 4.4 Mentor Sources and Actions to Take

MENTOR SOURCE	MENTOR RECIPIENT	ACTIONS TO TAKE
Professional learning network	Librarian Library professional	Adopt practices, continue to read and learn about modification of current practices.
Librarian Library professional	Young library users (tweens and teens)	Model library use among community members of all ages. Create opportunities for students to lead and demonstrate what they have gained as a result of active participation in library spaces.
Teen literacy leaders	Younger readers/ community members	Facilitate community conversations about important books. Advocate for continued and improved library programming.

Mentorship

Librarians who serve tweens and teens can also benefit from working with mentors personally, professionally, and especially in terms of evaluation and assessment. Mentors can answer questions or offer advice on how to conduct ongoing assessment, as well as provide unfiltered feedback on your work and programs. Seek out mentors in other types of libraries and even in other public-serving fields who will help inform your practice and aid in program creation, evaluation, and assessment.

Valerie has relied on mentors from public libraries and community college/university library systems on a myriad of topics, including evaluation and assessment. She went back to some of her mentors while writing this book and asked them what advice and recommendations they had for librarians conducting program evaluation and assessment. Their responses are shared below.

LIBRARIAN SPOTLIGHT

kYmberly Keeton, Chief Artistic Officer of Novella Media, LLC

kYmberly is also founder of ART | library deco, a virtual African American art library and repository. She was named the ALA Emerging Leader and *Library Journal* 2020 Mover & Shaker.

kYmberly believes that "involving representatives from the youth to help gauge data is an asset. Using social media and videos (like Zoom) is a great way to get feedback from a first-person perspective." When asked what tools she recommends for reporting results and recording data, she had this to say: "It depends on what I am looking at as it pertains to the type of program. I believe that using a creative approach to evaluating this type of information is a good way to do this and include all data that is comprehensible to the project. I think that using a web platform is a great idea! You are able to show your entire program and how it formed[,] then discuss the reporting and evaluation data."

LIBRARIAN SPOTLIGHT

Kiera O'Shea Vargas, Former Community College Library Director and current information PhD student at the University of South Carolina

Kiera's go-to tool for program evaluation and reporting those results is the DEI Scorecard, developed by the COD committee, which ALA has recently implemented. She had this advice for librarians (particularly those who serve tweens and teens) regarding conducting program evaluation and assessment:

"I would remind librarians about the importance of diversity. Oftentimes when librarians center on collections material and/or programming, they fail to implement diversity. This is because many fail to understand what true diversity and equity is based on their personal biases. When working on evaluations and any type of assessment, the ability to be objective is key."

---○---

A large part of learning to provide exceptional library services to teens is those we learn from and those we surround ourselves by. For Julia, developing a professional learning network of individuals whom she has mostly come to know online has been a crucial part of her development as a student of library and information services, a literacy educator, and a library professional.

The next section spotlights some of the mentors who have helped Julia along the way, and who are excellent examples of school librarianship at its finest.

LIBRARIANS MAKING NOTABLE CONTRIBUTIONS TO THE FIELD

Suzanne Sannwald's (@suzannesannwald) school library website (westhillslib.weebly.com) shares the importance of providing digital spaces that are as complex and multifaceted as our physical spaces when it comes to student outreach—particularly during the uncertainty of living through a global pandemic.

Julie Stivers (@BespokeLib) is the cofounder (along with Kathryn Cole) of #LibCollab, an online professional learning network of librarians who come together to share resources and discuss best practices.

Mary Thomas, a teacher-librarian in D.C., has continued to advocate for libraries and young people in tangible ways. Her display skills are unmatched, and she has taught me so much about how to use digital tools to continue to bring library services to young people in innovative and meaningful ways during the pandemic. Read an interview with Thomas that appeared on the Overdrive blog (bit.ly/3uhuhPb).

School librarians **Ashleigh Rose** and **Jillian Heise** stand as active examples of anti-racism in library spaces with the courage to advocate for and incorporate titles into their collections, along with programming that supports these titles in the face of community backlash and defunding, which is a constant struggle. Rose shares her library refresh experience in this BookSource blog post: bit.ly/368jVZV. Heise, who started #ClassRoomBookADay, describes the reading challenge on her blog heisereads.com.

Dr. Betina Hsieh (@ProfHsieh), **Dr. Sarah Park Dahlen** (@readingspark), and **Dr. Jung Kim** (@jungkimphd), discuss the importance of actively and continuously seeking information about Asian representation in a library collection, as well as better ways to include programming that centers on Asian identities and experiences. It isn't enough to just add books to the collection. We must continually educate ourselves about the nuances of Asian representation even and especially if our library user populations are not dominated by people of the Asian diaspora. Read a post by Dr. Kim on Dr. Bickmore's YA Wednesday blog bit.ly/3Is4ZCW

Two librarian mentors of Julia's—without whom she would not have been able to build her library—are **Janet Damon** and **Suzi Tonini** from Denver Public Schools EdTech and Library Services. Both appeared on the Heinemann podcast to discuss culturally responsive librarianship (bit.ly/3irmecI) and libraries as healing spaces (bit.ly/3JHtOfH).

Edith Campbell's blog (edicottonquilt.com) offers a wealth of information about not only African American representation in books, but how to continue to look for the books that are not necessarily given multimillion-dollar marketing budgets—but that may be of high interest for our students, nonetheless.

Dr. Debbie Reese (@debreese) is one of the foremost scholars about the representation of Native Americans in children's literature, alongside children's book author and scholar **Cynthia Leitich Smith**, whose website shares resources for Native American children's and young adult books: bit.ly/3tokrLR.

Key Points

Once you've designed your library program, the work has really just begun. Continued efforts will have to be made to ensure staffing continues beyond your tenure and to make sure your learning extends beyond those in your immediate environment. Advocacy efforts are more than conducting user surveys and sharing results with school staff and the extended community. They must be shared with student users, as well, so they can see the type of literacy community they've constructed taking a shape, not just for the here and now, but for the future, as well. Online professional networks are a wonderful way to showcase exciting moments happening in library spaces, but also to continue to build community.

- Collect demographics information in collaboration with collection development specialists in order to best meet the needs of your user population. Don't have a collection development specialist? Reach out to library district collection development specialists for an adjacent area with a library population similar to yours.

- Continuously reflect on the sources of your inspiration, as well as how you can continue to diversify them in terms of their backgrounds and experience as well as their contributions to the field.

- Develop an ongoing mentorship model so young people understand the importance of adding to existing conversations and contributing their thoughts about how library spaces can be improved.

- Connect to professional learning networks and follow librarians and library hashtags online. AASL has a list of suggested hashtags to follow (standards.aasl.org/project/hashtag-bank).

Reflection

- How do you currently collect data on library programs and report it?

- What new tools and innovations can you incorporate to facilitate data collection and analysis in regard to library programming?

- Consider expanding your professional learning network online and in person to incorporate new trends and best practices in librarianship, as well as program evaluation and assessment.

CHAPTER 5

Programming Ideas & Curriculum Connections

Much has already been written about practical programming or the intersection between theory and practice, so you may find yourself wondering, what new information does this book offer? Our intention is to speak from the lens of our experience and to provide ideas that might level librarianship up from what has been done and what is often expected to explore new areas of possibility. We offer some information from basic primers, as well as ways to expand cultural relevance and foster resilience, support emotional well-being, and activate students as they aspire to use the skills they develop in library spaces to work toward a new type of society more concerned with mutual care and collective consciousness.

Practical Programming Template

Librarians have exponential demands on their time. The idea of creating and developing programs that are fresh or cutting-edge can be quite daunting. The template below can help narrow the focus in terms of program development and serve as a means to brainstorm programming ideas. Create this programming template in a favorite working platform that can be easily accessed and referred to in order to streamline your thinking around programs.

A completed and fleshed-out template like this can be presented to library directors and other stakeholders in pitches for funding and in presentations such as state of the library or upcoming library plans.

Table 5.1 Practical Programming Template

PROGRAMMING QUESTIONS	RESPONSES
How many programs a month?	
What standards will these programs address (i.e., ISTE, AASL, state education standards, college readiness standards, etc.)?	
What type of programs do my students want?	
What are the learning and technology skills needs of the community you serve? How can programs directly and positively impact those needs directly?	

Continued

PROGRAMMING QUESTIONS	RESPONSES
What technology tools can I utilize to make the program a success from promotion and execution to evaluation and assessment?	
What are the trends in literature, education, and popular culture that can lend to programming?	
What partners within and outside my institution/organization can I connect with to make a program a success?	
What are the social, emotional, cultural, and linguistic needs of your community, and how can library programming address those needs?	

When designing programming, it can help to take a backward design approach. Think of the essential questions or learning that students and patrons will take away from library programs and look at a season, quarter, or a whole academic school year in advance to plot out programs and timelines (McTighe & Wiggins, 2005). Place the programs on a calendar that is publicly available so administrators and stakeholders know what is going on in the library and when.

From a curriculum and instruction/educational leadership perspective, consider the book *Understanding by Design* by Grant Wiggins and Jay McTighe when developing your program plan. Be flexible and open to change! You are not married to your program plan. As we have seen over the last few years with the COVID-19 pandemic, circumstances can change quickly and librarians may have to reschedule or modify programs to make them virtual.

Considerations for Certified Teacher Librarians

It is often said that school librarians operate as silos on their campuses. Unless a school librarian is lucky enough to work in a large high school with like-minded, innovative, forward-thinking, and culturally competent colibrarian(s) and library staff, they are usually the only ones on the school campus working in that role. College and public librarians are fortunate in that they may work with a team of other librarians and library staff to develop and carry out programming, share ideas/learning, as well as promote/advertise and create program assessments.

This is why it is essential for school librarians to develop a PLN or community, particularly one centering on programming in person and online, as many librarians and consultants share ideas and information on platforms such as Twitter and YouTube.

Suggestions for Building Your PLN

The "lists" feature on Twitter is extremely helpful, as users can create lists and add key content creators to them, then check the lists frequently to stay updated.

On YouTube, the "subscribe" feature is also a way to follow key content creators in the programming space and instructional technology space.

Consultants such as Desiree Alexander of Educator Alexander Consulting release videos frequently on instructional technology using Google Apps and other popular technology tools, teaching and instruction, educational leadership, and much more that can be useful in program development, execution, and evaluation.

In creating programs, consider state standards for content areas and college readiness. Obtain print or digital copies of state standards and library standards, and bookmark the digital standards sites for quick reference. The AASL Standards book is an essential manual for school librarians and is available in the ALA online store, as well as at their conferences. The AASL Standards website is helpful in providing librarians with resources for application to daily practice.

Cultural Competence & Library Program Development

In addition to attending professional development sessions on cultural competence, and culturally relevant and responsive education that a school district or an institution may provide, reading in the field will aid in developing, executing, promoting, and assessing and evaluating programs. Consider the title *Information Services to Diverse Populations* by Dr. Nicole Cooke. Cooke provides a primer to librarians working in various types of libraries on providing library services to diverse populations, touching on everything from marketing and outreach to evaluation and assessment. This can inform your work in programming development and ensure that information about programs reach and teach communities in an increasingly global world whose information and educational needs are ever-changing.

Considerations for School Library Staff

As mentioned in chapter 4, there is a trend that involves school planners and administrators staffing libraries with library professionals or "technicians," rather than those certified as teacher librarians or traditionally trained in MLIS or MLS programs. What this means for the future of school libraries is uncertain. However, it is clear that students still need access to quality physical materials, programming, and virtual collections that nurture their intellectual, creative, and inquisitive minds. It is possible to develop exemplary library programming without traditional knowledge or skills of librarianship as long as there is knowledge about and respect for the fact that an important part of any library professional's job is to provide access to information, resources, and technology that transform lives.

Hirsch's "2017 NMC Horizon Report–Library Edition" identifies several "big picture themes" that will impact information organizations, their services, and their value over the next five years." (p. 3) The following list is adapted from the list of themes:

- Library professionals will remain the gatekeepers of information and knowledge.

- Library professionals should instruct young people in the use of new media and technology.

- Library professionals will need to place greater emphasis on user design and accessibility in order to serve their communities effectively.

- Library professionals tasked with instruction will need to become aware of and proficient in the use of culturally relevant and sustaining practices.

- Library professionals will need to emphasize the development and implementation of a framework for understanding digital fluency and literacy.

- Library professionals will need to reimagine organizational structures and balances of power to more equitably distribute between youth and adults due to the fact that so much information young people want is readily accessible. The adult's role shifts from becoming a purveyor of information to supporting the development of critical consciousness and deeper metacognitive skills that often culminate in social activism and engagement.

To meet these challenges, librarians may need to focus on different skills. Table 5.2 shares some essential skills for today's librarians.

Table 5.2 Essential Skills for Library Professionals (adapted from Hirsch)

ESSENTIAL SKILLS FOR LIBRARY PROFESSIONALS	NEW SKILLS AND COMPETENCIES TO CONSIDER
Soft Skills • Critical thinking • Independence, time management, multitasking • Collaboration • Professional networking (building a PLN) (See #LibCollab)	**User Experience** What types of interpersonal skills do we need to employ to make sure all library users feel welcome, regardless of their previous experiences with or comfort in library spaces? How can we protect the privacy of library users while still encouraging those of similar interests to find one another and collaborate?
Communication and Outreach • Advocacy • Communication skills • Marketing (see connecting with librarian communities chapter 4) • Presentation skills (see presenting student data chapter 2)	**Open Access** How can we more readily share materials and access to information with one another to avoid gatekeeping or elitism that can develop when some organizations have greater or higher quality resources due to funding sources, etc.?
Leadership and Management • Budgeting and fundraising • Change management • Crisis management • Leadership • Project management • Strategic planning	**Design Thinking** How does a library's physical space, as well as programming, reflect the needs of library users? What outside resources can be incorporated into a library program to lessen the distance that is often created between those who are working within a system and those who are not?

Continued

ESSENTIAL SKILLS FOR LIBRARY PROFESSIONALS	NEW SKILLS AND COMPETENCIES TO CONSIDER
User-Centered Mind-Set • Deep knowledge of diversity, equity, and inclusion in librarianship • Customer service • Reference and research • Library services management	**Creation Culture and Makerspaces** How might we include opportunities for students to create (works of art, clothing, literature, utilitarian items) via makerspaces in libraries without taking away from the central purpose of libraries, which is information browsing, access, retrieval, and dissemination?
Technological Skills • Data analysis (see analysis of circulation data) • Expertise with databases and library collection management systems	**Data Analytics** How can analysis of circulation and user data (such as languages spoken or other demographic information) help a library become more efficient and integrated with a school's mission and vision? How can it help support the development of a school-wide community culture of inquiry and literacy?

Media Literacy for a New Era

When Julia became a school librarian, one of the most important things to her about the job was to make sure she circulated physical materials in a collection that had been allowed to grow stagnant, with many titles that were old and not particularly of interest to the student population. What many (including her fellow teachers and administrators) were not able to conceptualize was that a library was a perfect place for exploring the importance and evolving nature of media literacy in their school systems and societies. According to *Information Services Today*,

"Teaching students to access, evaluate, and use information, both within their academic environment and as citizens of a democracy, is at the heart of the school library curriculum" (Hirsch, p. 72).

Therefore, it is so important for us to continue to see and build library spaces where young people learn to access, evaluate, and use information in ways that are relevant and applicable to the lives they live. So how do we know what information is needed? Keep in mind the following information from the ACRL Framework for Information Literacy:

- Authority is constructed and contextual (consider the Media Bias chart from adfontesmedia.com).

- Information creation is a process.

- Information (in all forms) has value.

- Research is a process of inquiry.

- Scholarship is a conversation with pre-existing knowledge.

- Searching is strategic exploration.

Information literacy is about building on a learner's competencies (the knowledge they already have). Therefore, we must identify the context in which they are learning and living, along with the skills and knowledge that are needed for that context, and then co-create lessons and systems of measurement that will build upon what they already know with a clear eye on what will be most useful to them. There is no one-size-fits-all media literacy curriculum. However, there are standards and the practical application of those standards (see table 5.2).

Table 5.3 Student Learning Standards

ALA Information Literacy Standards for Student Learning	Practical Application	Area for Growth
The student who is information literate … • accesses information efficiently and effectively • evaluates information critically and competently • uses information accurately and creatively	In school settings, we currently teach students to access information quickly and effectively using database subscriptions. We then practice evaluating information using tools like the CRAP (currency, reliability, authority, and purpose) test: bit.ly/3iksC5R.	Develop ways for students to use information that is accurate, creative, and relevant to the contexts in which they are consuming and creating content. An example might be students researching the connection between COVID-19 rates in their community, air quality, and the number of trees that have been planted.
The student who is an independent learner is information literate and … • pursues information related to personal interests • appreciates literature and other creative expressions of information • strives for excellence in information-seeking and knowledge generation	In school settings, we currently teach students to pursue information related to prescribed topics that are sometimes student selected, but there is a very narrow limit to the literature students are encouraged to appreciate.	Look for what is worthy of academic study in the texts students choose to read or those that closely match genres they are naturally exploring and expanding ideas of what "excellence" means together with students. For ideas, visit disrupttexts.org.

Continued

ALA Information Literacy Standards for Student Learning	Practical Application	Area for Growth
The student who contributes positively to the learning community and to society is information literate and ... • recognizes the importance of information to a democratic society • practices ethical behavior in regard to information and information technology • participates effectively in groups to pursue and generate information	In school settings we often see students accessing information as practice in response to the call of a particular assignment. We remind them about the importance of ethical behavior sometimes by simply telling them they are not allowed to use certain sites (e.g., Wikipedia) or threatening to use plagiarism checkers. Students actually collaborate quite a bit in virtual spaces. During the height of the COVID-19 pandemic, when virtual school was normalized, many students felt they had to collaborate in virtual spaces (such as Snapchat) because they had no other place for social connection.	Why not leverage the natural propensity young people have to collaborate and maximize their ability to use the information they acquire for the betterment of the communities and societies in which they live? See the blog post Julia wrote on "Activating Community and Social Engagement Through Digital Citizenship" (bit.ly/36bLDEZ).

Currently, we spend most of our time teaching basic research skills and giving students the opportunity to practice evaluating the resources they find.

A progression of this would be to help students evaluate context and consider different information needs for different contexts. This is similar to what students of literature do when they evaluate the effectiveness of an author's style or tone for a particular audience.

A true transformation of practice would result in students who know how to consume information in responsible ways and are discerning and aware of the motives of the sources that produce any particular content.

Finally, students will create content that reflects an awareness of audience, context, and previously existing knowledge, as well as the ways their contributions add to established conversations (figure 5.1).

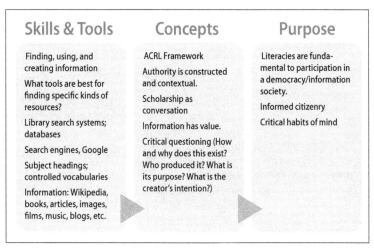

Skills & Tools	Concepts	Purpose
Finding, using, and creating information	ACRL Framework	Literacies are fundamental to participation in a democracy/information society.
What tools are best for finding specific kinds of resources?	Authority is constructed and contextual.	
Library search systems; databases	Scholarship as conversation	Informed citizenry
Search engines, Google	Information has value.	Critical habits of mind
Subject headings; controlled vocabularies	Critical questioning (How and why does this exist? Who produced it? What is its purpose? What is the creator's intention?)	
Information: Wikipedia, books, articles, images, films, music, blogs, etc.		

Figure 5.1 Skills + Concepts + Purpose (modified from Wilson's General Model, 1999)

Teen Advisory Councils

When creating leadership roles for young people in libraries, so much of what we tend to come up with is (in a way) performative. We tell students they can choose books for a community book club, for instance, but we limit their choices to titles that are "school appropriate" or that will, in other words, not make adults uncomfortable. We've often heard of the phrase "getting comfortable with discomfort," but what does that actually mean for adults when it comes to sharing power with young people?

Many of us have library helpers or assistants. Some students even get academic credit for serving in these roles. But even if a student receives a grade for helping out in the library, is that as good as it gets? We have the professional responsibility to consider whether systems give students power in ways that will allow them to transform library spaces and processes for the betterment of those around them, or if we are merely allowing them to make small decisions within the confines of what we adults have determined is acceptable.

With respect to teen advisory councils, there are several ways power can be extended beyond simply running the circulation desk, reshelving books, helping to order, or running a book club. Table 5.4 shares a few examples.

Table 5.4 Advance Your Teen Advisory Council by Looking at Current Practices and What's Possible for the Future

CURRENT PRACTICES	FUTURE POSSIBILITIES
Checking books in and out for peers	Curating collections for peers
Reshelving books	Studying and conducting yearly evaluations of classification systems
	Sharing experiences with staff
Requesting books for orders	Blogging or researching books that might be ordered
	Reading, rating, and reviewing ARCs of new titles
	Conducting interviews or informal surveys with community members about favorite titles

Continued

CURRENT PRACTICES	FUTURE POSSIBILITIES
Running book clubs	Consider book clubs with thematic/social-justice components
	Co-create and conduct needs assessments with library staff to see what books or other materials community members would like to explore collectively with others
	Read and learn about methods for holding critical conversations
	Develop new policies and practices for school systems after reading related works

Bringing It All Together

When we think about student advisory councils and expanding the circle of community, it is perhaps best to quote the late bell hooks, who wrote in *Teaching Community: A Pedagogy of Hope*:

> Dominator culture has tried to keep us all afraid, to make us choose safety instead of risk, sameness instead of diversity. Moving through that fear, finding out what connects us, reveling in our differences—this is what brings us closer, what gives us a world of shared values, of meaningful community. (p. 197)

We can in fact build this loving community when we focus on sharing stories and experiences around the resources libraries provide and the people within them—without forgetting about those who do not necessarily feel library spaces are for them. Library professionals have to remember accessibility for those who have internalized the harmful narrative that reading is something to be done only for a grade, only when assigned, or only if the practice comes easily to us.

Students should absolutely be encouraged to contribute their individual voices and experiences to that of a collective student body, but also understand that their stories and experiences are part of a continuum of voices and stories that existed before them and will continue long after they have graduated or moved on. All too often, adults propose the idea that the skills and content we teach will be useful to future generations. The truth is that the future holds possibilities we can hardly know. What will remain is the human propensity for connection, curiosity, and innovation. This is fundamentally the reason why libraries as spaces for the preservation, collection, curation, and dissemination of information must be safeguarded and maintained.

 ## LIBRARIAN SPOTLIGHT

Lovie Howell, Librarian at Benton Middle School in Benton, Louisiana

One of the most rewarding library programs that I have ever been a part of was adopting the Daraja Children's Choir as a school, linking this to International Dot Day, and seeing the results of connecting the dots.

Daraja Children's Choir is a group of 9–13 year old's from Uganda who travel to America annually to tour, learn more about themselves as leaders, and take that back with them to Uganda and their families and communities. Before the choir arrived in the US, each class adopted a choir member. They displayed their photos in their classes, had written and video correspondence back and forth, and learned about Ugandan culture. This was all facilitated by the library, where they could also come to learn Ugandan language, upload their videos, etc.

Along with these activities we also shared the book, *The Dot* by Peter H. Reynolds with the choir members and their interns (aunties and uncles for the tour). Those choir members sent us their "dots," which we proudly displayed in our library before their arrival.

When it was finally time for the choir to visit our school for the day, we were fortunate that Terry Shay, the creator of International Dot Day heard about what we were planning. He graciously contacted Peter H. Reynold's publishing company, which in turn was thrilled to send each choir member their very own copy of *The Dot*. In addition, Peter H. Reynolds sent sent bookplates to be placed in each book.

Upon arrival, the Daraja Choir was met with a fanfare of students yelling their names as they got off their tour bus to enter the school. You see, our students "knew them" and were so very excited to see the child they adopted and learned about. After a schoolwide assembly with the choir sharing their music with us, each child was presented their very own copy of *The Dot* by their adopted class's teacher. Pictures were taken and sent to the publishing company, Terry Shay, and Peter H. Reynolds so they could see how the dots were being connected from Uganda to Lousiana, to Massachussetts, to Iowa.

The rest of the school day each choir member was able to spend a typical day with each adopted class. Lunch in the cafeteria was a Daraja member favorite along with recess, P.E., and of course Library. I am not sure I have ever been as overwhelmed by a lesson as I have been by this particular one. The culminating effort of Ugandan and American children reading *The Dot* is a video I watch over and over and will continue to share forever. We truly all were abundantly blessed by our students and the Daraja Children's Choir students during this experience. It is by far one of the proudest moments I have had as an educator.

Book Clubs

From Oprah to bookstores to local public and school libraries, book clubs are an ever-popular form of programming that draws readers and thinkers of all ages. Book club themes and possibilities are infinite, and the manner of meeting—in-person meetings and/or virtual discussions—help to make book clubs a flexible and popular library program. The immense popularity of young adult literature, particularly over the last fifteen years or so, make YA themed book clubs the perfect springboard with which to build tween and teen library programming. Managing a book club allows for teen voice and input to guide book choices, discussions, and activities. Teens' insight and input can not only bolster book club popularity but help sustain it.

How to Get Started

Start by looking at popular student- or youth-led book clubs online and in your community. These clubs can positively impact literacy among teens and give them voice and ownership over their reading choices. As a result, the books and the stories are a direct reflection of the students who are reading them.

In education, the focus has always been on what is considered the canon of English literature, like Bronte's *Wuthering Heights* and classics such as *The Catcher in the Rye* by Salinger, and while those titles are still widely read and studied in high schools and universities, why not have students read, discuss, and study the plot, characters, and rising and falling action of novels that are popular today and feature characters that are just like them?

As part of its mission, We Are Kid Lit Collective "looks for ways to improve the literacies of Indigenous and People of Color (IPOC) children, promote books written by and about IPOC, and to encourage gatekeepers to bring a lens of critical literacy to their work" (We Are Kid Lit Collective, 2022).

 We Are Kid Lit Collective
(wtpsite.com)

Reading lists from We Are Kid Lit Collective, as well as YALSA and state book lists, can serve as an excellent source for librarians to not only learn about new middle grade and YA titles but to share them with tweens and teens so they can take part in selecting titles as book club reads.

When meeting in person, librarians host monthly in-person book club meeting discussions once or twice a month, providing refreshments, and teens are encouraged to share major themes, insights, and personal learnings from the books.

When conducting online meetings, Valerie often uses pictures and images and poses questions from reader's guides, then presents them to club members using Microsoft Sway. Sway presentation formats allow the presenter to zoom in and bring focus to images and text, which makes it an excellent technology tool to drive discussion in book club meetings.

Another popular tool for book clubs is the inclusion of activities, crafts, and cosplay events for meetings. Librarians can provide supplies or create kits that teens can pick up for activities and crafts to be done during book club meetings. For a *Hidden Figures* book discussion, Valerie found some great wooden airplanes on Amazon that club members could easily assemble and decorate. Airplanes and the science behind how airplanes work were a major part of the book *Hidden Figures*, so it was a perfect tie-in to the book club discussion.

Cosplay events, especially for manga book club participants, were also extremely popular with the teens Valerie worked with at Woodrow Wilson High School in Dallas, Texas. At Woodrow, she typically held meetings after school and when they did cosplay, she allowed time for students to change from their school uniforms to their cosplay outfits. One caveat that she gave students was to remember that they were on campus and not at a comic con, so to please dress appropriately! But other than that, the students were able to express their creativity and talk about their favorite characters and series through the cosplay events.

Parent Permissions

When Desiree Alexander was a high school librarian, she had parents sign a book club permission slip that stated that students were reading titles that may include adult themes and issues that may be deemed controversial. Students read everything from the classics to new releases in school-library-based book clubs (this was long before the issues of censorship that have come to the forefront in 2021). Be sure to not only obtain parent permissions but to engage parents in book club activities and discussions. Tweens and teens can learn from the insights and life experiences parents may share from reading various titles.

Book Reviews and Expanding Your Circle of Community

When looking to expand a circle of community, we always begin with *self*. That's a human tendency and a reflection for many of us of being socialized in countries where individualism is prized over collectivism (figure 5.2). One way to reverse this is to have conversations about the ways students are rewarded in a school community for collectivism or individualist behavior. An example of this was given in the table above: rather than rewarding an individual with a grade or participation points for serving as a library assistant, why not form a teen advisory board and redistribute power so the true reward is collective advancement?

Individualism

1. Fostering independence and individual achievement

2. Promoting self-expression, individual thinking, personal choice

3. Associated with egalitarian relationships and flexibility in roles (e.g., upward mobility)

4. Associated with private property, individual ownership

Collectivism

1. Fostering interdependence and group success

2. Promoting adherence to norms, respect for authority/elders, group consensus

3. Associated with stable, hierarchical roles (dependent on gender, family background, age)

4. Associated with shared property, group ownership

Figure 5.2 Individualism vs. Collectivism

When students in Julia's library community do book reviews, it is typically within the Follett Destiny Discover system, and students create these book reviews in order to contribute to the overall desired community culture of reading and sharing. There have been times when teachers made the book review assignment part of the student's overall grade or points for the day, but this is due to the fact that we are still operating in a society that commodifies learning and too many students have internalized the notion that they should not do any task without some sort of material reward. Grades are academic currency and a part of the system of punishments and rewards that we have somehow not managed to completely move away from.

Alternative Ways to Measure Grading and Further Considerations

 Sarah Zerwin has been a long-time advocate of alternatives to traditional grading practices. Her work is also featured on the blog thepapergraders.org that details her exploratory journey with several other teachers in her learning community.

 Joe Feldman's *Grading for Equity* gives the basics of how grading practices that are "accurate, bias-resistant, and motivational [and] will improve learning, minimize grade inflation, reduce failure rates … and create stronger teacher-student relationships and more caring classrooms."

 José Vilson writes about race, class, and education through stories from the classroom and researched essays. His rise from rookie math teacher to prominent teacher leader takes a twist when he takes on education reform through his eponymous blog, theJoseVilson.com. He calls for the reclaiming of the education profession while seeking social justice.

Literacy Instruction

Student achievement data and collaboration with instructional coaches, teachers, and administrators are essential in program design from a literacy instruction perspective. Principals usually develop a "state of the school" presentation for staff in which they outline the student achievement picture of the school, present the school's campus improvement plan, or plan for continuous improvement, then detail what school staff will do in terms of literacy instruction and improving student achievement in all areas of a school.

Librarians should be part of that plan and part of the discussion of how to continually improve the literacy skills of students so students move from reading capacity that is considered to be below or at grade-level literacy to postsecondary literacy, so students will continue to be successful while on the high school campus and long after graduation.

Valerie finds that librarians have to insert themselves into discussions around literacy instruction and present their plans and programs that will support it. Inserting the library and the librarian is not easy, as the school library is often an afterthought to some school leaders, rather than a forethought. Librarians often have to just show up to leadership team meetings they may not have been invited to or attend professional learning community meetings they are not expected to be present at. However, this will push administrators' thinking from the library being an afterthought to being vital.

Engaging parents in literacy instruction during the tween or teen years can also be a challenge, but in teaming with the parent/community liaison, programming can be developed so parents are part of the literacy instruction process. Parent engagement events, like parent academies or workshops held in the evenings and hosted by the school library and school librarian in conjunction with parent and community liaisons and post-secondary education-advancement organizations based in schools, can serve as a catalyst in driving literacy instruction and parent engagement during the tween and teen years.

In addition to book clubs as part of a library literacy-instruction programming plan, library guest speakers and workshops for students and the community can also play an important role in that they provide students access to professors, poets, actors, and community members they otherwise may not encounter. Professional organizations such as NCTE, ALAN, YALSA, and AASL—and the conferences and workshops they present—can also inform and provide librarians with resources to bolster literacy instruction in schools.

Advocacy Matters

As mentioned in previous chapters, advocacy for libraries must continue. It is a deliberate act of suppression of intellectual freedom when library spaces are defunded, and the only way that libraries will survive, in whatever future form they may take, is if young people and future generations see their worth.

In *Social Justice and Cultural Competency: Essential Readings for School Librarians,* Sabrina Carnesi states that the library is a site for social justice. She says that, according to the mission put forth in the AASL (2009) national guidelines, school libraries exist to ensure students are "critical, effective, empowered, and ethical thinkers and users" (p. 8). Through the lens of Rioux's (2010) fifth assumption, "The provision of information services is an inherently powerful activity. Access, control, and mediation of information contain inherent power relationships. The act of distributing information is itself a political act" (Rioux, 2019, p. 13). Therefore, when we limit library funding, resources, and spaces, or attempt to exercise too much control over the ways in which students can function in library spaces, we are essentially acting in oppressive ways that will have far-reaching consequences.

So, how do we begin to advocate in ways that are organized and effective?

Effective Advocacy Practices

1. Co-create with students whenever possible. This includes conducting regular needs assessments and being transparent with them about the results.

2. Determine who is at the top of any power structure, and be honest with young people about what it will take to get the individual or individuals to meet their demands or requests.

3. Practice open dialogue with community members, and research ways of communicating across lines of difference.

4. Support student leaders who regularly facilitate conversations about social and organizational transformation. Bring them into your spaces to model and share their experiences with younger, less experienced students.

5. Interrogate your systems to determine whether student leadership is authentic or optical and performative.

6. Engage in dialogue about the role(s) of tradition and nostalgia in shaping curriculum.

7. Develop an authentic media literacy curriculum that has the end goal of social critique and/or contribution in mind so students can put their learning to use in the real world.

Conclusion

The practical ideas shared are an excellent catalyst for getting programs started and sustaining them. However, in reviewing book lists, scheduling programs, creating assessments, and evaluations, be sure to keep a pulse on the community you serve.

Get the input of tweens and teens every step of the way as you brainstorm, plan, and develop programs. Tweens and teens can be the biggest advocates for libraries and library programs, particularly when they are confident that their voices, ideas, and creativity are heard.

The importance of library and technology education professional organizations cannot be underscored, as librarians can look to these organizations for ideas, tools, and resources for all aspects of programming. Partnerships with organizations and businesses and grants can help make programming plans a reality and even bolster programs—from funds to purchase supplies to people who can serve as volunteers, and guest speakers for program events.

After program evaluation and assessment, keep in mind the data you want to collect and present to decision-makers in your community, and take an academic research approach. In assessing learning from programs, take a curriculum design approach to crafting assessments.

Communicate the benefits of library programming on literacy and skills that teens can transfer to the workplace, as many of the teens we serve are working right now to support themselves and their families. They can also learn and develop skills they will take into their chosen profession and studies after they leave K–12 education. Engage parents in library programming, inviting them to be part of the discussion so tweens and teens can learn from them, as well.

Our ultimate goal is lifelong learning and the ability for the tweens and teens we serve to reach their personal, professional and educational goals, as well as spark creativity and ingenuity. What better way to do this than to create meaningful and impactful library programs and services that help young people do just that!

Key Points

Practical programming must move beyond the circulation of materials and the traditional roles librarians and library professionals have demonstrated, because the role of the librarian is constantly changing. One of the most profound changes of the last ten years is the role that critical media literacy must play in our instructional practices, as well as professional skills and knowledge development. As we think about teen advisory councils and ways to expand communities of literacy beyond the walls of a school building, we should also keep in mind the overall purpose of libraries: to be places of intellectual freedom and exploration where, as Jorge Luis Borges wrote in his acclaimed work *The Library of Babel*:

> The library will endure; it is the universe. As for us, everything has not been written; we are not turning into phantoms. We walk the corridors, searching the shelves and rearranging them, looking for lines of meaning amid leagues of cacophony and incoherence, reading the history of the past and our future, collecting our thoughts and collecting the thoughts of others, and every so often glimpsing mirrors, in which we may recognize creatures of the information. (1962)

Other takeaways from this chapter:

* Redefine the role of library professionals as funding and policies around school libraries shift.

- Consider the role of library professionals as advocates for intellectual freedom and supporters of independent reading as an area of curricular study.

- Consider critical media literacy as a cornerstone of library coursework and a vital component students will need to participate in an ever-evolving technological society.

- Teen advisory councils and book reviews are ways to build communities of readers that go beyond the walls of a physical building and beyond the relatively few years a young person spends within a formalized school system.

- Continue to advocate for libraries as a public resource, ensuring they exist and meet the specific needs of all individuals.

- When we redistribute power so students are truly able to co-create library spaces, everyone benefits and the effects are long-lasting.

Reflection

- Since library policies and librarian roles are changing, are you part of the leadership team on your campus or in your institution? If not, how can you get a seat at the table to advocate for your role, programs, intellectual freedom, and the right to read?

- In addition to welcoming students and meeting student needs, how can you ensure libraries are a resource for the community they serve?

- How can student voice and student agency be amplified in the library?

References

American Association of School Librarians. (2022). AASL
  Standards framework. standards.aasl.org/framework/

American Association of School Librarians. (2022). Standards
  crosswalks. standards.aasl.org/project/crosswalks/

Asmar, M. (2021). Denver is considering closing three schools to
  make way for a new Montbello High School. bit.ly/3N8pEPI

Boggs, Grace L. (2016). *Living for change: An autobiography.*
  Minneapolis, MN: University of Minnesota Press.

Borges, J. L. (1962). *The library of Babel.* Boston: David R. Godine.

Chang, S., Penney, L., Wardrip, P., Anderson, A., Craddock, I.,
  Martin, C. K., Millerjohn, R., & Stone, N. (2019). *Opportunities
  and vignettes for library makerspaces.* bit.ly/3KUcwfa

City of Cedar Hill. (n.d.) The Zula B. Wylie Public Library.
  cedarhilltx.com/2053/About-the-Library

Coates, Ta-Nehisi. (2015). *Between the world and me.* Melbourne,
  VIC, Australia: Text Publishing Company.

Cooke, Nichole A. (2016). *Information services to diverse populations:
  Developing culturally competent library professionals.* Santa
  Barbara, CA: ABC-CLIO, LLC.

Dankowski, T. (2020). Ridding schools of reading trauma:
  Tips for interrupting traditional practices and diversifying
  collections. americanlibrariesmagazine.org/blogs/
  the-scoop/116407/

DiMaggio, T. (2020). Healing reading trauma at #ALAVirtual20.
  bit.ly/3qhYmN1

Ewing, Eve L. (2019) Mariame Kaba: Everything worthwhile is
  done with other people. bit.ly/3IszUyZ

Ferlazzo, L. (2017). Interview: Culturally sustaining pedagogies. bit.ly/3IqM1ML

Gonzalez, N., Moll, L., & Amanti, C. (Eds.). (2005). *Funds of knowledge: Theorizing practices in households, communities, and classrooms.* Mahwah, NJ: Routledge.

Hicks, T., & Turner, K. H. (2015). *Connected reading: Teaching adolescent readers in a digital world.* National Council of Teachers of English.

Hirsh, S. (Ed.). (2018). *Information services today: An introduction, Second Edition.* Lanham, MD: Rowman & Littlefield. scholarworks.sjsu.edu/faculty_books/209

hooks, b. (1994). *Teaching to transgress: Education as the practice of freedom.* Oxford, UK: Routledge.

hooks, b. (2003). *Teaching community: A pedagogy of hope.* Oxford, UK: Routledge.

Institute of Education Sciences. (n.d.) Teacher characteristics and trends. nces.ed.gov/fastfacts/display.asp?id=28

Institute of Museum and Library Services. (2022). The school librarian investigation: Decline or evolution? libslide.org

International Literacy Association. (2019). *Advocating for Children's Rights to Read.* bit.ly/3CXrHSj

Kachel, D. E., & Lance, K. C. (2018). *Why school librarians matter: What years of research tell us.* bit.ly/3tpISsw

Ladson-Billings, G. (1995). Toward a Theory of Culturally Relevant Pedagogy. *American Educational Research Journal, 32*(3). bit.ly/38z30jZ

McTighe, J., & Wiggins, G. (2005). *Understanding by design.* Alexandria, VA: Assn. for Supervision & Curriculum Development

Mardis, M. A., & Oberg, D. (Eds.). (2019). *Social Justice and Cultural Competency: Essential Readings for School Librarians*. Santa Barbara, CA: ABC-CLIO, LLC.

Miller, D. (2009). *The book whisperer: Awakening the inner reader in every child*. Hoboken, NJ: Jossey-Bass.

Montiel-Overall, P., Nuñez, A. V., & Reyes-Escudero, V. (2015). *Latinos in libraries, museums, and archives: Cultural competence in action! An asset-based approach*. Lanham, MD: Rowman & Littlefield.

Orenstein, C. (2003, December). Women of the year 2003: Carla Diane Hayden. msmagazine.com/dec03/woty2003_hayden.asp

Radaganthan, R. S. (1931). *The five laws of library science*. London: Edward Goldston.

TED Conferences, LLC. (2021). How to discover your "why" in difficult times. bit.ly/3uVSvig

TEDxBoston. (2012). About Time: Marlon Carey at TEDxBoston. youtube.com/watch?v=sc7iROGlK4Y

Thakur, M. (2021). Noname's transition from rapper to librarian: Marking the opening of the Radical Hood Library. bit.ly/3KZ0qSb

Thiong'o, Ng'ugi Wa. (1986) *Decolonising the mind: the politics of language in African literature*. Melton, Woodbridge, Suffolk: James Currey.

Wolf, M. (2018). Skim reading is the new normal, and the effect on society is profound. bit.ly/3KXJNq0

Worth, S. (2019). This library takes an indigenous approach to categorizing books. bit.ly/3N8u3T6

Index

A

AASL Standards, 10–11, 13, 109
"About Time" (Carey), 22
ACRL Framework for Information Literacy, 113
adults, actions to take, 74–76
advisory councils, teen, 94, 116–119
advocacy, 86–87, 127–128. *See also* marketing and library program advocacy
African American representation, 101
"Akwaaba librarianship," 26
ALA Information Literacy Standards for Student Learning, 114–115
Alexander, Desiree, xi–xii, 108, 123
Alim, Sammy, 57
Amato, Jared, 121–122
anti-racism, 100
art shows, 28
Asian representation, 100–101
assessments. *See also* program evaluation and assessment
    needs, 42–43
    reading, 78
assimilation, 28–29
authentic assessments, 78

B

Bastrop Public Library (Texas), 21–22
Benton Middle School (Louisiana), 63, 119–120
Between the World and Me (Coates), 86
Boggs, Grace Lee, 36–37
book clubs, 75–76, 121–123
book fairs, 70, 75
book reviews, 124–125
books
    library science laws, 91
    music preferences and, 49
    readers, matching with, 79
Books Love Art, 28
Borges, Jorge Luis, 130
Brian Deer system, 46
budgeting, 72–73
Burks, LaMoya, 54–56

C

Campbell, Edith, 101
Carnesi, Sabrina, 127
Cary, Marlon, 22
change, 43
Charles, Cynthia, 52–54
"Children's Rights to Read" (International Literary Association), 18–19
choir, Ugandan, 119–120
circle of community, 124
circulation, 85
classification, 44–46
clubs, student, 26
Coates, Ta-Nehisi, 86
collaboration with college librarians, 56
collection management, 85
collectivism, 124
college librarians, 51–56
communication, 111
community, building, 28–29
community, circle of, 124
Connected Reading (Hicks & Turner), 89–90
Cooke, Nicole, 109
cosplay events, 123
Counting Opinions platform, 92
COVID-19 pandemic, 11
creative, getting, 76–80
crowdfunding, 63
cultural awareness, 31
cultural blindness, 30
cultural competency, 30–32, 35, 109
cultural incapacity, 30

Index

cultural proficiency, 31
culturally relevant librarianship
  about, 29–30
  cultural competency, developing,
    30–32
  questions to ask yourself, 30
  readings, 32–34
  resources, 34
  Staff Diversity Reading Challenge,
    35–36
culturally relevant pedagogy, 29
culturally responsive library space
  classification, 44–46
  displays, 48–49
  environment, physical/virtual, 48–51
  programming, 46–48
  scorecards, 47–48

D

Dahlen, Sarah Park, 100–101
Dallas Public Library, 93
Damon, Janet, 69, 101
Daraja Children's Choir, 119–120
data collection, 89–91
demographics, 83–84, 88
Denver Public Library, 68, 87
Dewey Decimal classification system,
  44–45
Dietrich, Bethany, 21–22
Dillard University, 52–53
displays, 48–49, 73
dominator culture, 40, 118
donations, 70, 75
Donors Choose, 63
The Dot (Reynolds), 119, 120

E

environment, physical/virtual, 48–53, 86.
  See also welcoming environment
ethnic/racial demographics, 83–84
evaluation. See program evaluation and
  assessment

F

5D displays, 73
501(c)(3) organizations, 64
flexibility, 22–23, 41–43
Follett Destiny Discover system, 124–125
Freire, Paulo, 79
funding, 61–65, 67
Future Ready Librarians, 12–13

G

Garrett, Kiara, 49
Ghana, 26
grading practices, 125
grant reporting, 65
grant writing, 62

H

Hayden, Carla, 68
Heise, Jillian, 100
Hicks, Troy, 89–90
Hidden Figures, 122–123
Hirsch, Sandra, 110, 112–113
hooks, bell, 39, 40, 118
Howell, Lovie, 63, 119–120
Hsieh, Betina, 100–101

I

imagination, capturing, 6
independent reading, 18
individualism, 124
information literacy, 113–115
Information Services to Diverse Populations
  (Cooke), 109
Information Services Today (Hirsch), 112–113
inquiry, role of, 6
intellectual spaces, libraries as, 84–86
interests, student, 5–6
International Dot Day, 119–120
International Literary Association, 18–19
ISTE AASL and Future Ready Librarians
  crosswalks, 12–13
ISTE Standards for Educators, 11–12

J

Junior Librarians program, 38

K

Kaba, Mariame, 17, 43
Keeton, kYmberly, 98
Kim, Jung, 100–101
Klein Oak High School (Spring, Texas),
    28, 65

L

labeling, 73
Lambert, Nancy Jo, 35–36
language, 46
Lankford, Daniela, 28, 65
leadership and management, 111
learning, advancing/deepening, 6–7
liberatory consciousness, 1–2, 79–80
librarians
    college, 51–56
    in literacy instruction, 126, 127
    role of, 16
    school, 74–75, 108–109
    stereotypes about, 16–17
    tasks, 84–86
librarianship
    "Akwaaba," 26
    culturally relevant, 29–36
    laws of, 91
libraries. *See also specific topics*
    culturally responsive, 44–51
    as growing organisms, 91
    as intellectual spaces, 84–86
    public, 27, 60–61, 92–93
    purpose of, 130
    school, 27, 60
    times tweens/teens use, 25
library helpers/assistants, 117
library legacies, reimagining, 16–17
The Library of Babel (Borges), 130
library professionals/"technicians,"
    109–112
library programming. *See also* specific
    topics

budgeting, 73
culturally responsive, 46–48
effective, 5–7
inclusive, 1–2
online, 11, 15
revolution in, xi
scheduling, 14–16
school culture and, 20–22
standards and, 9–14
sustaining for everyone, 80
template, 105–107
why, starting with, 7–9
library skills, lifetime, 36–37
literacy instruction, 126–127
literacy standards, 114–115
Little Free Libraries, 73
Living for Change (Boggs), 36–37
local funding, 64

M

makerspaces, 66–68, 88
management, 111
marketing and library program advocacy
    about, 68–69
    budgeting, 72–73
    donations, 70
    surveys, user feedback, 68, 71
material purchases, 72–73
Mayor's Teen Council, 27–28
media literacy, 112–116
mentorship, 97–101
Microsoft Sway, 122
Miller, Donalynn, 18
mind-set, user-centered, 112
mission statements, 6–7
Model of Connected Reading, 89–90
Montbello branch (Denver Public Library),
    68, 87
music, 49

N

National Education Association, 35
National Education Statistics, 83
national funding, 64–65

Native American representation, 101
needs assessment, 42–43
networking, 64
non-authentic assessments, 78

O

online programming, 11, 15
oppressed, 36–37
"others," 39–41
outreach, 111

P

parents, 123, 126–127
Paris, Django, 57
partnerships, 92–94
pedagogy, culturally relevant, 29
professional learning networks (PLNs), 96,
    97, 99, 100, 108
program evaluation and assessment
    about, 88–89
    assessments, creating, 94–95
    data collection, 89–91
    partnerships, 92–94
    reporting format, 92
    research approach, 94–95
    STEM and makerspaces, 88
    template, 95
    tips, 98–99
programming. *See* library programming
public libraries
    partnerships with, 92–93
    standards, 60–61
    tween/teen experience of, 27

R

racial/ethnic demographics, 83–84
Radaganthan's Laws of Library Science,
    89–90
Radical Hood Library, 45
readers
    adults as, 75–76
    books, matching with, 79
    engaging, 76, 77–78, 79
reading

assessments, 78
connected, 89–90
independent, 18
rights, 17–19, 40
standards, 10–11
tastes and habits, 42, 68, 71
Readington Middle School (Bridgewater,
    NJ), 38
Reedy High School (Frisco, Texas), 35–36
Reese, Debbie, 101
resource sharing, 85
Reynolds, Peter H., 119, 120
right to read, 17–19, 40
Rose, Ashleigh, 100

S

Sannwald, Suzanne, 100
scheduling, 14–16
school culture, 20–22
school librarians, 74–75, 108–109
school libraries, 27, 60
Shay, Terry, 120
signage, 73
Sinek, Simon, 7
Singer, Stephanie, 38
"Skim Reading Is the New Normal, and
    the Effect on Society Is Profound"
    (Wolf), 77
SLIDE report, 74
Smith, Cynthia Leitich, 101
social justice, 44, 127–128
Social Justice and Cultural Competency
    (Carnesi), 127
social media, 87, 96
soft skills, 111
Sonic Drive-In, 63
Staff Diversity Reading Challenge, 35–36
stakeholders, 20
standards
    AASL Standards, 10–11, 12–13, 109
    about, 9–10
    ALA Information Literacy Standards for
        Student Learning, 114–115
    ISTE AASL and Future Ready Librarians

crosswalks, 12–13
ISTE Standards for Educators, 11–12
no standards versus, 60–61
public libraries, 60–61
school libraries, 60
STEAM/STEM, 66–68, 88
Stivers, Julie, 75, 100
student agency, 26–28
subjugation, 28–29
surveys, 20, 68, 71

T

Teaching Community (hooks), 40, 118
technological skills, 112
teen advisory councils, 94, 116–119
templates
    program assessment, 95
    programming, 105–107
Texarkana College, 54–56
Texas Municipal League, 27–28
Thomas, Mary, 100
3D displays, 73
time, flexibility of, 22
times tweens/teens use libraries, 25
Tonini, Suzi, 101
#TrueBookFairs, 70, 75
Turner, Kristin Hawley, 89–90
"2017 NMC Horizon Report–Library
    Edition" (Hirsch), 110

U

Ugandan choir, 119–120
user-centered mind-set, 112

V

Vargas, Kiera O'Shea, 99
virtual library environment, 86

W

We Are Kid Lit Collective, 121–122
welcoming environment
    about, 25
    college librarian perspectives, 51–56
    culturally relevant librarianship, 29–36

culturally responsive library space,
    44–51
flexibility, 41–43
library skills, lifetime, 36–37
"others," creating understanding/
    connection with, 39–40
philosophy for creating, 26–29
why, starting with, 7–9
Will W. Alexander Library, 52–53
Wolf, Maryanne, 77
Woodrow Wilson High School (Dallas), 123

Y

youth-serving organizations, 93–94

Z

Zula B. Wylie Public Library (Cedar Hill,
    Texas), 6–7

CPSIA information can be obtained
at www.ICGtesting.com
Printed in the USA
JSHW010016030623
42541JS00004B/5